WICKED

CHARLESTON

VOLUME 2

WICKED

CHARLESTON

VOLUME 2

PROSTITUTES, POLITICS AND PROHIBITION

MARK R. JONES

Charleston London
History
PRESS

Published by The History Press
Charleston, SC 29403
www.historypress.net

Cover Image: The Library of Congress

First published 2006

Manufactured in the United Kingdom

ISBN 1.59629.134.6

Library of Congress Cataloging-in-Publication Data

Jones, Mark R. (Mark Rowell), 1959-
Wicked Charleston. Volume II, Prostitutes, politics, and Prohibition /
Mark R. Jones.
p. cm.
Includes bibliographical references.
ISBN 1-59629-134-6 (alk. paper)
1. Charleston (S.C.)--Moral conditions--History--19th century. 2.
Charleston (S.C.)--Moral conditions--History--20th century. 3.
Prostitution--South Carolina--Charleston--History. 4. Prohibition--South
Carolina--Charleston--History. I. Title. II. Title: Prostitutes, politics,
and Prohibition.
HN80.C43J66 2006
975.7'915--dc22
2006009814

CONTENTS

ACKNOWLEDGEMENTS

First of all, a thousand thanks to the staff at The History Press—Kirsty, Amanda, Hilary, Brittain, Julie, Jason and everyone else for helping to make my first book, *Wicked Charleston: The Dark Side of the Holy City*, such a success. Thanks for paving the way for the sequel, guys.

Once more, thanks to all the Doyles at Palmetto Carriage Works for bringing me into the tourism industry. They have been most supportive in giving me a flexible work schedule that allows me the freedom to pursue other interests. Tom, Tommy, Ben, Anne Marie and Mary Alice...thanks.

Thanks to John LaVerne of Bulldog Tours for being the best kind of boss; he gives his tour guides the freedom to be creative. Bulldog Tours is the best walking tour company in Charleston because all John wants is the best tour guides who give the best tours. I'm proud to be part of that elite group.

Speaking of tour guides...I have the pleasure of working with some of the best, not only at Bulldog but also at Palmetto Carriage. I believe that being a Charleston tour guide is a privilege that should not be taken lightly and I strive to infuse that spirit in my fellow guides. A good tour guide is an ambassador to the city. In Charleston, there are no bad tours, only bad tour guides. I work hard not to be the latter.

Thanks to the staffs at the Charleston Library Society, the South Carolina Historical Society, the South Caroliniana Library and the South Carolina Room at the Charleston County Public Library for all the time and effort. I know it's your job, but not everyone with a job is as pleasant as all of you.

Thanks to Gary Dow, proprietor of The Tavern on Coates's Row for the information, the tour and the incredible photo. Gary owns one of Charleston's greatest treasures: a three-hundred-year old liquor store.

Once again I have to mention J. Francis Brenner—the old codger himself—who is still going strong in his nineties. Thanks for the information *and* the inspiration.

Thanks to Jim Brain, friend, tour guide and man about town, for his sage advice and counseling. Like a lighthouse in a hurricane, Brain creates good space with his beacon of wisdom.

Thanks to Rebel Sinclair, author of sweat-inducing romance novels (*The Devil of Charleston* and *Spirit of the Shadows*), tour guide extraordinaire and the best of friends. Also known as Kari, she is patient, passionate and an inspiration to those of us who *really* know her. With Rebel, it's never "what you see is what you get," it's always more, and *always* surprising. Life is always interesting with Rebel around.

Last, thanks to Judge Waties Waring for his courage. As I researched his life and learned more of the scorn and tribulations heaped upon him, I came to admire his implacable devotion to his vision…even when the entire "genteel" city was against him, making his life a living hell. He lived a daily life of personal courage against a social storm of resentment that is so resonant, it inspired me to begin living the rest of my life the way I needed to.

AUTHOR'S NOTE

The closets in Charleston are deep, wide and securely locked, with many skeletons that will never see the light of day. *Wicked Charleston, Volume 2* continues the search for as much of the dark side of the history of Charleston as I can uncover, so far.

While I was researching *Wicked, Volume 2*, I discovered how protective some of the city can be of its so-called "genteel" heritage, particularly one organization that dates its formation in Charleston to 1801. This organization has incredible resources of the most famous and historic tavern in Charleston, and I wished to include some of their visual material in the book. But they refused permission. I had a discussion with the head of the local chapter, and he seemed interested until I mentioned that part of the book dealt with the issue of prostitution in Charleston. He said, "You're not going to associate prostitution with us, are you?" I answered, "It's not my intention, but I follow where my research leads me."

Later that day he called back and told me that he had called the national board in Washington, D.C. "We want nothing to do with *your* book." This book is a bit less than it could have been with their participation. What a shame people can be so shortsighted.

While promoting the first book, *Wicked Charleston: The Dark Side of the Holy City*, I had the pleasure of meeting many supportive local residents. I also had the pleasure of meeting some not-so-supportive SNOBs and SOBs. One particular incident stands out. I was at the Historic Charleston Foundation on Meeting Street, a store that stocks only non-fiction and photographic books about southern history. While I was sitting at my table a Charleston blue blood "lady" walked in and said, "Oh, you're the one who wrote *that* book." She then picked up a copy of *Wicked Charleston* and held it the way most of us would hold a bag of vomit. "I didn't know they sold fiction in this store," she said. "You do know *none* of this is true, don't you?" To which I replied, "Ma'am, you're just afraid that your family's name will show up at some point."

She dropped the book on the table and walked away. Obviously, for some locals, it's all right to be rude to those you see as your inferiors. Likewise, I also know it's all right for the rest of us to be rude to those who assume they are our superiors.

I have already begun knocking on closet doors, looking for dusty skeletons, and collecting information for what could be *Wicked, Volume 3*. I'm also looking forward to meeting more of my superiors. Until next time...

CHAPTER ONE
POLITICS AND PROSTITUTES

The city is full of three types of people, the first being soldiers, the other classes are politicians and prostitutes, both very numerous, and about equal in honesty and morality.

Charleston Mercury, December 19, 1860

EAT, DRINK AND BE WITH MARY

In 1692, William Penn, founder of Pennsylvania, wrote to the English Lords Proprietors that Charles Towne had become "a hotbed of piracy." As a Quaker, Penn was also outraged by the behavior of the wayward women who frequented the taverns; he urged civic leaders to address the situation. The Carolina state assembly ignored Penn's complaints. However, one year later there was an entry in the 1693 *Journal of the Commons House of Assembly* that ordered three women "who frequented a tap room on The Bay [East Bay Street] and infected a goodly number of the militia with the pox" to be deported from the state. They were sent by boat to Philadelphia. Take that, you Quakers!

Charles Town was one of the busiest port cities in the colonies by 1720. There were often more than 150 sailing vessels from Portugal, Spain, England, France, Italy and the Caribbean at dock in the Charles Town harbor. With an average of twenty sailors per ship, that translates to an influx of three thousand men in the city roaming the streets in search of one thing: entertainment, usually in the guise of wine, women and song. Soon a thriving hotbed of taverns, bordellos and gaming houses were catering to the needs of sailors, backwoods fur traders, militia and locals along Bay, Elliott, Union (State), Chalmers, Queen and Cumberland Streets. All these men were looking for a place to eat, drink and be with Mary.

One of the earliest brothels was located on Union Alley (currently 17 Chalmers Street, the Pink House), which today is an art gallery. The small three-story Pink House was built by John Breton out of Bermuda stone before 1712. The building consists of one room per floor with the first floor used as a tavern and working girls on the second and third floors. When one walks up the narrow wooden staircase to the second and third floors today, it feels cramped and claustrophobic, due to the very low ceiling. Many people instinctively lower their heads and hunch their shoulders as they stand in the third floor room. Keep in mind that people were much shorter in the eighteenth century than they are today. Besides, how many times was a man actually standing up on the third floor?

The Pink House later became a law office. What a perfect transition. Nothing changed except the hourly rates went up. The main difference between a lawyer and a prostitute is that the prostitute won't charge you after you're dead.

The Charles Town nightlife brought so much increased rowdiness and violence that many citizens, led by cabinetmaker Thomas Elfe (whose workshop still stands at 54 Queen Street), wrote a letter to the city complaining that these Ladies of Eden were spreading disease and disrupting their commerce. It didn't help matters that more than thirty members of the Night Watch sold "Juggs of Liquor to Seamen & Negroes" while on duty. By the 1760s there was a dramatic increase in the "vagrants, drunkards...notorious bawds and strumpets and idle persons roaming the streets, swearing and talking obscenely." Mary MacDowell of Pinckney Street was cited for keeping "a most notorious brothel" and for "harboring loose and idle women." Even the assembly criticized the "superabundance of licensed Taverns and Tippling Houses, gaming houses and disorderly houses."

Deitrick Olandt's tavern was described as "an improper and disorderly house" because he maintained several females "in the upper portion of his house." Cornel June's brothel at the corner of State and Guignard Streets (near the current location of Palmetto Carriage's Big Red Barn) was denounced for keeping "between six and fifteen white women in service against their will."

Many of the ship's captains and factors tried to keep the sailors out of the brothels lest the ships would lack a full crew when the tide and wind were ready. Rarely did the law ever interfere with the operation of a brothel. One of the only recorded instances of police action against a brothel was when a patron was robbed of his wallet, which had been left on the floor in a pair of quickly discarded trousers.

A DRINKING TOWN WITH A HISTORICAL PROBLEM

In 1830, the average American man consumed fifty gallons of liquor per year. That number does not include beer. In Charleston, the rate was higher. Carl Bridenbaugh of Boston wrote, "The importation of liquors at Charleston Town staggers the imagination — 1500 dozen (18,000) bottles [of ale]...1219 hogshead [wine]...and 58 barrels of rum." This was a six-month supply for one modest tavern.

Gentlemen were encouraged to drink; in fact, part of *being* a gentleman meant holding your liquor. Having the reputation of being a "three-bottle man" was a mark of excellence. A "three-bottle man" consumed at least three bottles of whiskey or wine per day. Again, that did not include beer, which was consumed in the same manner as modern soft drinks.

Just before the outbreak of the Revolutionary War the assembly became concerned that the Night Watch could not contain the "growing Vice and Immorality." The assembly, however, did little to solve the problem. They merely ordered the loose women to move from the waterfront district to an area four blocks west called Dutch Town, as it was settled mainly by Germans. Within the shadow of the St. John's Lutheran and Unitarian church steeples, the six-block section of Clifford, West, Beaufain, Logan and Beresford (Fulton) Streets soon became a "constant scene of nightly brawls and riots."

In 1780, during the British occupation of Charles Town, orders were posted for soldiers to avoid bawdy houses. Several of the Ladies of Eden were shipped out of the city for "health reasons" but most of the houses did a booming business where the soldiers found "willing female companionship." Soldiers were always good for the bordello business. Lucky for the madams, the men of Charleston started a war against Yankee aggression in 1861. More on that subject later.

The governor and his council tried in vain to regulate the sale of liquor. The selling of intoxicants was "observed to be mischievous and to impoverish the otherwise sober planters." The laws also tried to limit the amount of credit a tavern keeper could extend to customers. Ignoring the liquor laws became a long tradition in the Lowcountry.

Taverns were much more than drinking establishments; they were prominent social institutions. Taverns hosted political functions. Men's clubs and other charitable organizations held their meetings in the building.

Up until the 1760s, most of the beer consumed in Charles Town was imported from Philadelphia, Liverpool, or Bristol, Connecticut. There was a real need for a local brewer, but few men in the city had the skills, until Edmund Egan arrived.

Egan was born in England and was an apprentice under a London brew master before his arrival in Charles Town. He encountered trouble setting up business. First, he was a newcomer with no reputation or references, making it difficult to arrange the financial credit needed to procure brewing equipment. He supported himself for a few years as a fencing master and also went into a factoring partnership with Nathanael Greene and William Coates.

In 1765, when the passage of the British Stamp Act ignited a passionate support of American manufacturing, Egan found a partner with John Calvert. They announced that a Charles Town brewery was now in production. They advertised the sale of "Doubled brewed Spruce beer, table and small beer." They also offered to ship any quantity above five gallons.

Two years later, Parliament passed the Townshend Acts, which forced another round of boycotts against England by the colonists. Egan had trouble getting quality hops and malt. In 1770, Egan was able to import his own barley seeds and convinced some local planters to lay in a crop, and one year later, Charles Town had their first constant supply of local brew. By 1775, Egan was outselling all import brews in Carolina. According to 1772 financial records Egan's income was almost £20,000.

His brew house had two brick vaults forty-one feet by thirteen feet. The malt house and kiln were one hundred feet by twenty-two feet. Egan employed eight Negroes: two coopers who built casks and kegs and six brewers. He also had two "house wenches" on the property.

During the Revolution, Egan tried to expand his business by building a distillery on Coming Street, which failed and was abandoned. After the war, Egan borrowed money from William Gibbes to establish a new brewery, but he died before the venture could be completed.

During the years preceding the Revolutionary War, Christopher Gadsden and the Sons of Liberty met at Shepheard's Tavern. Charles Shepheard built his tavern at the corner of Broad and Church Streets in 1720 and it quickly became the most important public house in the city. In 1734, Shepheard's hosted the first theatrical season in America in the Long Room upstairs. Two years later, on October 28, 1736, the first meeting of the Ancient and Honorable Society of Free and Accepted Masons took place in the tavern. And later, in 1801, the Supreme Council of the Thirty-third Degree of the United States of America was opened in the Long Room.

One interesting club was called Club Fourty-Five. On November 21, 1772, a group of the Sons of Liberty met at the Liberty Tree at Mazyck's pasture to swear their defense against the tyranny of the British. The tree was decorated with forty-five lights and forty-five skyrockets were fired. Forty-five men paraded down King Street to Broad Street to Dillon's Tavern. Forty-five lights were placed upon the table, along with forty-five bowls of punch and forty-five bottles of wine, which were then consumed.

Captain Thomas Coates purchased a row of waterfront structures in 1804 and persuaded his wife, Mrs. Catherine Coates, to open her establishment on the corner. Mr. Coates also purchased the Pink House on Chalmers Street. When Mrs. Coates's By the Bay, as it was called, opened (at the current corner of East Bay Street and Exchange Street), it was considered to be one of the finest taverns in the city. The business exhibited what was considered to be the best collection of wax figurines in America, including replicas of George Washington, Dr. Ezra Stiles (late president of Yale College), David and Goliath and others. After Mrs. Coates's death in 1824, the tavern was closed. At some point it was the Oceanic Cafe and was replaced with a liquor store in the late 1890s, which is currently still open for business.

The location on which Coates's Tavern stood currently houses a liquor store called The Tavern, complete with a subterranean basement. Archaeologists from Colonial Williamsburg, the Universities of South and North Carolina and from the Tower of London have examined the brickwork in the basement and they agree that the masonry work is common of southeastern England of 1550–1650, making it plausible that the current structure dates as early as 1710. There are remnants of a brick fireplace, which indicates that at one point the basement was used for cooking to serve the customers of the tavern on the upper floor. The archways in the basement at one time were the openings for doors that led to a tunnel beneath East Bay Street to the Cogswell, Walker and Evans building that sits directly across from the tavern. Due to the constant cool temperatures in the basement, through the years it has been used as a wine cellar and vegetable dry storage.

During Prohibition, the building housed the offices of an insurance business, which was nothing more than a front for a bootlegging operation. It is entirely plausible that on this location alcohol has been served for almost three hundred years.

Many taverns had colorful names. Some of the more colorful through the years included Old Slaughter, the Cock Tavern, the Cock Pitt, the Salutation and the Cat, the Mourning Bush, the Mitre and the Devil, the Crown and Anchor, the Star and Garter, the House of Quality, the Suckling Pig, the Knock Down and Drag-Out, the Robber's Inn and the Bucket of Blood.

In the late eighteenth century, due to the arrival of French refugees from Santo Domingo, taverns were being challenged in popularity by French coffeehouses. However, most people believed coffee did far greater harm to a person than did rum, whisky, brandy and beer. Some taverns even took out newspaper advertisements extolling the virtues of liquor and the ill effects of coffee. The coffeehouse merchants fought back and published pamphlets of the benefits of the genteel practice of drinking coffee.

Coffeehouses may have experienced an ebb and flow of popularity through the decades, enjoying resurgence during the 1960s and the recent impressive phenomenon of Starbucks, but liquor has always been in fashion in Charleston, even when it was illegal.

THE 1860 DEMOCRATIC CONVENTION

The first non-military shot of the Civil War was fired in Charleston at the Democratic Convention of 1860. The Democrats were split between two factions (abolitionists and pro-slavery) and the choice of Charleston as the location to host the convention was, at best, inept. Robert W. Johannsen, in his book *Politics and the Crisis of 1860*, wrote:

POLITICS AND PROSTITUTES

No American political convention has ever held so much meaning for party and union as that...which gathered in Charleston...Upon the decision at Charleston rested not only the future of the Democratic Party but also the continued existence of the Union.

The choice of Charleston as the site of the convention was foolhardy. The Democratic Party that met in 1860 was deeply divided by one issue: slavery. Stephen Douglas was the clear favorite of Northern Democrats, while the Southerners demanded that the Democratic Party come out with a platform in clear defense of slavery. The decision to hold the convention in Charleston (the largest slave importing city in the United States and the most ardent defender of the institution) has to rank as one of the worst decisions in American political history. It may have *sounded* like a good idea to hold the party's convention in a Southern state. The hope was that this symbolic act of "healing" would help win the region in the election and solidify the Union. They were wrong. Compared to the 1860 Charleston Convention, the 1968 Chicago Convention was a love fest.

The convention convened on April 23 and the Southern Democratic delegations began to press their long-rumored plan to walk out unless a plank that called for passage of a federal slave code was included in the party platform. Then, there were the "fire-eaters," a group of Southern Democrats who actually wanted the Republican candidate to win the election, thus hastening the secession of the slave states.

The weather during that last week of April 1860 was not unusual for the Lowcountry: hot and muggy with daytime temperatures hovering in the mid-nineties and nighttime temperatures remaining in the eighties. The heat inflamed an already edgy population and was an irritant to the visitors already in a bad mood.

Charleston was not a large city and had never hosted a national party convention before. The city was not centrally located and physically could not support such a large gathering. Hotel accommodations were limited and hotel owners had colluded to fix higher prices during the convention. Transportation problems were monumental. One passenger had to change trains six times between Washington and Charleston. Franklin Pierce, delegate to the convention, wrote, "I have never been taught to believe in eternal damnation, but if it exists, the journey to Charleston has given me the only sample I shall ever need."

Fifteen hundred Douglas delegates from various states took over the Mills House Hotel, at five to six people per room. They also rented

Hibernian Hall and set up 132 cots in the main room. The Charleston Hotel housed the more radical secessionist delegates.

What followed was the longest and most divisive political convention in United States history. The two factions of Democrats were so badly divided that fistfights broke out among the delegates in the hall and in the surrounding taverns and streets. Gunshots and knives were pulled by delegates during heated debates on the convention floor. The delegates from New York, Pennsylvania and Massachusetts arrived in Charleston on luxury steamship liners and stayed on board in their staterooms. The New York delegation, knowing the reputation of Charleston, arrived with thirty barrels of whiskey and "forty women of questionable character." The Pennsylvania delegation arrived with two hundred cases of ale and thirty-two "amiable females." The Massachusetts delegation—the Puritans!—arrived with no alcohol and no women. Some things never change.

On December 19, 1860 the Charleston *Mercury* wrote, "The city is full of three types of people, the first being soldiers, the other classes are politicians and prostitutes, both very numerous, and about equal in honesty and morality."

After a riotous week, the convention went through fifty-four ballots but Douglas failed to achieve the necessary ⅔ of the votes. Forty-five delegates from nine Southern states walked out. The convention adjourned without a presidential nominee. They reconvened in June in Baltimore, where Douglas was nominated. As in Charleston however, the Baltimore convention was disrupted by a delegate walkout. This time, the walkout delegates decided to meet separately and nominate their own presidential candidate: Vice President John C. Breckinridge of Kentucky. Breckinridge ran as a Southern Democrat and won 18 percent of the vote and carried eleven states. Douglas won 29 percent of the vote but carried only one state. Abraham Lincoln, the Republican, was elected, setting the stage for the formation of the Confederate States of America.

THE LADIES OF EDEN

During the War Between the States many of the taverns in the city closed due to the scarcity of liquor; however, the bordellos remained opened for business. Confederate officers were supposed to be protecting the city, but spent most of their time in bars, brothels and gambling dens. Apparently these officers and gentlemen felt it was their duty to keep a close eye on the women, just in case some of them might turn out to be Yankee spies.

In a city already notorious for its wanton behavior, "free colored street walkers and loose white women impudently accosted passers-by. Gambling saloons were opened and drove a thriving business. Both officers and men were swept away by the same current of vice."

The city assembly passed a law "closing all bar rooms in which liquor is retailed." In February 1862, Colonel Johnson Hagood established a military police to prohibit "all distillation and sale of spirituous liquors." Because the law was routinely ignored, often by the military police themselves, it was finally lifted and the nightlife continued with the whorehouses, brothels and bordellos all doing booming business. The differences among a whorehouse, a brothel and bordello are of quality and price, with the whorehouse being at the bottom rung of the ladder.

Most prostitutes that were arrested were usually called by their first and last names in an effort to publicly shame them. However, it had little effect, and was often viewed by the women as free advertising—a way to create their reputation. There are instances of several madams being upset and angry with judges and newspaper editors for leaving out the name of the house in the court document or the news account. Free publicity was free publicity.

After 1836 prostitutes were classified as vagrants, a misdemeanor, not to be heard by general sessions court. Many court documents that list "female vagrants" are referring to prostitutes. Until 1860, the punishment for vagrancy was to be sold as an indentured servant until the fine was paid, or thirty-nine lashes and banishment.

However, the keepers of bawdy houses were to be tried by judge and jury. Madams accounted for 15 percent of antebellum court indictments.

THE BIG BRICK

Grace Piexotto was "a notorious woman who kept the worst kind of brothel for years, where harlots of all shades and importations break the quietude of night with their polluted songs." She was also the daughter of Selomoh Cohen Peixotto, the chazzan (music leader) of Beth Elohim synagogue. A good Jewish girl opened the most notorious brothel in the history of Charleston.

Grace's business, the Big Brick at 11 Beresford Alley (now Fulton Street), was "openly tolerated by leading men in of the city." Grace's girls at the Brick serviced white gentlemen, lower class sailors and ruffians, even free black men and slaves. In the capital of slavery the most integrated place was a brothel.

However, she did not like college boys and worried about the number of male students from the College of Charleston who were frequenting her house. She wrote a letter to the faculty requesting that they encourage the students to stop frequenting her business. She wrote, "They come early, stay late, have no money and get in the way of my paying customers."

John C. Fremont was one of the college boys that may have frequented the houses on Beresford Alley. Fremont was born on January 31, 1813, in Savannah, Georgia, and was expelled from the College of Charleston as a junior for "consorting with a mulatto wench." With so much free time on his hands Fremont became a constant visitor of the houses on Beresford Alley. Fremont was finally reinstated to the College, but he dropped out of school and in 1838 was commissioned second lieutenant in the Corps of Engineers, U.S. Army. During the following year Fremont was a member of the expedition that surveyed and mapped the region between the upper Mississippi and Missouri rivers. Between 1842 and 1845, Fremont led three expeditions into Oregon Territory. During the first he mapped most of the Oregon Trail and ascended, in present-day Wyoming, the second highest peak in the Wind River Mountains, afterward called Fremont Peak (13,730 feet). In 1843, he completed the survey of the Oregon Trail to the mouth of the Columbia River on the Pacific coast. The party, guided by the famous scout Kit Carson, turned south and then east, making a midwinter crossing of the Sierra Nevada Mountains.

Fremont attained the rank of major during the Mexican War (1846–48), and assisted greatly in the annexation of California. Later, he was appointed civil governor of California by the U.S. Navy commodore Robert Field Stockton, but in a conflict of authority between Stockton and the U.S. Army brigadier general Stephen Watts Kearny, Fremont refused to obey Kearny's orders. He was arrested for mutiny and insubordination and was subsequently court-martialed. After President James Polk remitted his sentence of dismissal from the service he resigned his commission.

In 1850, Fremont was elected as one of the first two senators from California. In 1856, he helped form the new Republican party and ran as its first presidential candidate, but was defeated by James Buchanan.

During the war Fremont was appointed a major general in the Union Army and put in command of the newly created Western Department based in St. Louis. On August 30, 1861, eleven months before the Emancipation Proclamation, Fremont issued an order that freed all slaves owned by Confederates. Abraham Lincoln was furious when he heard the news. Lincoln feared that this action would force slave owners in border states to join the Confederate forces. Lincoln asked Fremont to modify his order and only free the slaves owned by Missourians working for the South. Fremont refused. In 1864, Fremont was again a presidential nominee; he withdrew, however, in favor of President Abraham Lincoln. He later served as governor of the territory of Arizona from 1878 to 1883 and died in New York City on July 13, 1890.

In short, John Fremont helped map the Oregon Trail and founded the city of Fremont, California. He served as the governor of California and was one of the first two U.S. senators from California; he was the first man to run for president on the Republican ticket and became the first American official to free slaves. He later served as governor of Arizona. But he began by sowing his wild oats in Charleston whorehouses.

The Brick was constructed by Grace Piexotto in 1852 on a lot measuring sixty-two-feet-by-eighty-two-feet for which she paid $2,000. She subsequently built a complex of buildings in a courtyard arrangement: the still-standing three-story main building, a two-story and another three-story building. Well until the 1940s the Brick was the most prominent and notorious house in the city, the hub of prostitution. Grace once complained to the police chief about the treatment she was given. She commented,

> *I know that you policemen have to make your money on the side and that we have to pay you for protection, and that's all right. I know that you have to have a raid every once in a while and fine us, and that's all right. But there's one thing I object to. I object to you writing the charge against me for maintaining a disorderly house. I want to have you know that I have the most quiet, respectable, ladylike whores south of the Mason-Dixon Line.*

In fact, one of the ladylike whores of the Big Brick married quite well. Mary became the favorite consort of a Philadelphia gentleman who first visited the Brick during a business trip to Charleston. Soon, the Yankee gentleman was making trips to Charleston not for business, but for the pleasure of being with Mary. He finally brought her back home to Pennsylvania and introduced her to his family and friends. Mary was welcomed with open arms as a "charming, well-bred Southern lady"—another example of a Charleston whore sent to Pennsylvania, but this time she became the toast of the city.

The Big Brick made its way into infamy by inspiring an episode in Margaret Mitchell's Pulitzer Prize-winning novel *Gone With the Wind*, as well as the subsequent film. After the War Between the States, Charleston was under occupation by Union troops who were responsible for maintaining order. The streets were filled with "vagabonds, and scalawags who accosted the innocent." One afternoon two Charleston ladies driving a carriage back into town were waylaid in the area of the Charleston Neck by a gang of ruffians. The women managed to escape and complained to the authorities, but the Union troops did nothing to deal with the situation. Several Charleston gentlemen decided to take action. During the night a group of gentlemen attacked the camp of vagabonds in the Neck, killing several and running the others out of town. One of the gentlemen was shot during the attack. His friends carried him away, with Union troops in pursuit. The injured man was taken to the Brick where his wounds were cleaned and bandaged. The Union troops arrived at the Brick looking for the injured man. Grace promised the Union officer that all of these gentlemen had spent the entire evening with her girls and liquor.

In the film *Gone With The Wind*, Scarlett ignores Rhett's warning and drives alone to her lumber mill via the dangerous, black Shanty Town, filled with squalid tents and lean-tos. At the edge of Shanty Town, Scarlett is assaulted by two men (one white, one black), and then saved by her father's ex-foreman Big Sam. In the novel, Scarlett was mauled and nearly attacked by a black man.

That night, Scarlett's husband, Frank, along with Ashley Wilkes and other gentlemen, root out the band of vagabonds. Ashley is shot and carried home by Rhett Butler. When they arrive, Union officers are at the house, questioning the women about Mr. Wilkes' whereabouts. The men stagger into the house pretending to be drunk. The Union officer demands to know where they have been so the men admit they have been at Belle Watling's bordello during the evening, defusing the situation. Local Charleston tradition has always held that Grace Peixotto was the model for Belle Watling in *Gone With the Wind*.

The Brick also played a part in Wade Hampton's election to governor in 1876. When the Charleston Red Shirts supporting Hampton needed a place to meet without arousing the suspicion of the Union troops, they met in a room in the Brick, assured of complete privacy. It is quite fitting that a successful South Carolina political campaign operated out of a bordello.

Grace may have been the most loved (literally) woman in Charleston. When she died in 1883, the gentlemen of Charleston wished to pay their respects but of course, no gentlemen could attend the funeral of a madam! So, to honor her memory, the men sent an empty carriage in their place. According to tradition, Grace Piexotto had the second longest funeral procession in Charleston history—several blocks of empty carriages following the horse-drawn hearse. The longest funeral procession belonged to John C. Calhoun, congressman, U.S. senator, secretary of state, secretary of war and former vice-president of the United States. In Charleston, politicians and whores are honored on equal footing. How many cities honor a whore as grandly as they honor a former vice-president?

In the 1930s Ravin McDavid reminisced about the Brick:

> *One of the lamented institutions of Charleston is the Big Brick, number 11 Beresford Street, so-called because it was made up of large blocks of stone, of cement. The Big Brick, up until 1942 when the Navy, with the usual military gross disregard for local traditions, shut it down, was supposed to be the oldest whorehouse in continuous operation in the Western hemisphere. It had a very select clientele, and it used to pride itself on the dignity and propriety of its young ladies.*

McDavid remembers a story about the young Ashmead Pringle. Ashmead used to visit the Brick almost every Saturday night. As Ashmead was waiting for his favorite girl to be available his uncle arrived. Ashmead was astonished. "Why Uncle Ernest, what are you doing here?"

"Ashmead my boy, I might ask the same about you."

"You know boys will be boys, Uncle Ernest, but I always thought you and Aunt Agnes were happily married."

Uncle Ernest shook his head. "Well, now that you have found me here, I might as well tell you man to man, that I rather prefer the enthusiastic cooperation of these young maidens to the dignified acquiescence of your aunt Agnes."

MATTRESS GIRLS — THE OLDEST PROFESSION

By the turn of the twentieth century, Charleston streetwalking prostitutes had picked up the nickname "mattress girls," for the simple fact that they carried mattresses slung over their shoulders to accommodate their customers. They would find a dark corner of an alley, abandoned building, or a secluded spot in a nearby graveyard to lay out the mattress, conduct their quick business, roll up the mattress and go in search of another waiting customer. The more enterprising girls actually fashioned their mattresses to be worn over their shoulders with straps like a backpack, which alleviated the necessity of rolling and re-rolling the mattress, giving the girls more time to procure customers.

In 1901, the South Carolina Inter-State and West Indian Exposition was held on what is now Hampton Park. The Expo was attended by hundreds of thousands of international travelers, including President Teddy Roosevelt and Mark Twain. More than five million dollars was created for the local economy and the madams wanted to make sure they got their share. (And the men got theirs!) The madams united and published *The Blue Book*, a twelve-page pamphlet that listed houses of prostitution and the names of the Ladies of Eden employed at each house. One house advertised, "your trip to Charleston will not be complete unless you call at 37 Archdale Street." They promised that their customers would be "properly entertained." A transcript of *The Blue Book* appears in the Appendix.

In 1912, many locals believed the availability of brothels was actually a good thing since it "protected the respectable ladies in the city" from unwanted sexual attention. Prostitution was so readily available in Dutch Town that "on steamy afternoons Clifford Street so resounded with ribaldry flung from open window to open window by out-leaning women that shoppers on King Street stopped and looked." Other than brothels, another kind of house became popular, called an assignation house, where a room could be rented in half an hour increments. The usual way to identify an assignation house was by the miniature mattress hanging from the piazza.

The police organized token raids several times a year and made a few arrests so that they could claim they were cracking down on vice. A local businessman was enjoying a "special" lunch at a West Street bordello when it was raided by the police. To escape arrest, recognition, embarrassment and scandal, the gentleman jumped from the second story window to the alley below.

The building next door to the brothel had been damaged by the 1886 earthquake and listed to the left, while the brothel structure listed to the right. When the gentleman jumped from the window he became wedged between the two buildings about eight feet above the ground. He dangled naked with his bare legs kicking in the air and his buttocks in full view from the street. The fire department was called and he was rescued. And embarrassed when he was recognized and embroiled in a scandal.

The instances of assaults, robberies, gambling, stabbings and murders increased in the saloons and houses in Dutch Town and in the Market area. On Anson Street, a "low Negro dive" called the Eden Hotel, owned by George Williams Jr., was declared to be "a den of iniquity and vice." The members of St. John's Lutheran Church complained to the city about the mattress girls plying their trade along the front gates of the church. In fact, the church office for St. John's is sitting on the location of a former brothel, and over the entrance it reads: "Seek Ye First The Kingdom of God." I'm sure some of the patrons of the former business on this location probably thought that they had found heaven *before* it was church property.

The Law and Order League was one of the few voices of dissension against the tide of vice. They complained that many of the "assignation houses are run by Negro women for the use of white men and women. Charleston alone bears this unenviable reputation" and "Tradd Street was infested with Negro dives of the lowest kind whose orgies keep up all night."

In the 1920s, navy officials said the "incidence of venereal disease on the Charleston naval base was two to three times higher than [on] any other naval base." By the 1920s Market Street had become a thriving area for brothels and the city directory listed proprietors of bordellos as "Madam Belle Percival" and "Madam Mattie Sherman" but by 1930, the directory had dropped the 'madam" designation.

The police and madams began an understanding that the madams would post monthly bonds of $100 at police headquarters for the "right to maintain an illegal house of prostitution." The money went right into the city treasury. That's right. The madams paid the city for the right to operate an *illegal* brothel. The police were responsible for keeping health certificates up-to-date on each prostitute by ensuring that each woman had a weekly medical exam.

By the late 1930s Charleston's homicide rate was twice that of Chicago, and four times that of New York City. From January to November of 1930 there were twenty-two homicides in Charleston, but only two were brought to trial. The Charleston *Courier* said that "slashings and cuttings… [with] ice picks and open-blade razors, jagged broken bottles…are everyday occurrences. In Charleston it is commonplace for a man to lose his life over a woman…or a dime."

During World War II, military officials viewed venereal disease as a threat to the health of the servicemen. They called on Mayor Lockwood and the city council to eradicate prostitution in the city. The city's response was lackluster. Admiral W.G. Allen, commandant of the navy yard and Sixth Naval District, stated that "prostitution, the open sale of whiskey, gambling and the sale of 'dope' are now permitted without restriction." Admiral Allen then declared twenty-seven beer parlors on Market Street "off limits" to all navy personnel, and threatened to cancel all leaves in Charleston. Mayor Lockwood finally took some action. He closed down the "red light district," but the prostitutes just moved their activity to other locations, including gas stations, taxicabs and graveyards. But soon things were back to normal on Market Street.

In October 1942, the U.S. Army declared that the "city of Charleston is off limits for all personnel." That finally shocked the city into substantial action. In conjunction with military officials, Charleston police raided Market Street and arrested 626 prostitutes—346 white and 280 black. Nearly half were found to be infected with venereal disease. Nevertheless, the number of girls working the streets remained in the hundreds. Federal investigators cited "five brothels operating openly; call girls obtainable at two hotels and flagrant Negro commercialized prostitution." As late as 1947, federal records listed Charleston as one of fifteen cities in America where the vice conditions were deemed "unsatisfactory."

George Greene, who ran a business on Meeting Street on the block between Market and Hasell Streets (currently housing Aaron's Deli, Hyman's Seafood, Loose Lucy's and other shops), remembers several houses that "catered to sailors" along the block. Some of the working girls had a thriving second business: pickpocketing. The girls would easily lift the wallets from the drunken sailors, take the money and drop the wallets in the U.S. Post Office box on the sidewalk. Every Monday morning, the postman would pull "dozens of wallets out of the box" and send them back to the naval yard to be returned to the rightful owner.

POLITICS AND PROSTITUTES

There was also a hotel on Meeting Street that had three room rates. Five dollars would get you a room for the night. Eight dollars would get you a room for the night AND one hour with a working girl. Twelve dollars would get you a room AND a girl for the night.

By the 1950s, prostitution was segregated in Charleston for the first time in 280 years. Of the twenty-two houses on Market Street, only five catered to black men. The number of prostitutes remained over two hundred, which embarrassed Mayor Morrison. By 1960, most of the prostitution had been completely driven out of downtown to the north area, in closer proximity to the naval base, where it thrives to this day.

CHAPTER TWO
A WORLD TURNED UPSIDE DOWN

Outsiders gaze upon a Charleston election with wonderment, sometimes with merriment.

William Watts Ball

CARPETBAGGERS, SCALAWAGS AND YANKEE GOVERNORS

On February 18, 1865, Union forces entered Charleston. The black Fifty-fourth Massachusetts Infantry led the procession singing "John Brown's Body." Later that year Union General Robert Scott wrote, "The suffering among the people for want of food is almost indescribable and cases of insanity and death from actual hunger are reported in some Districts."

The Freedmen's Bureau was organized by the Federal government in 1865 for the purpose of protecting the freedmen in their relations with the whites. Chief functions of the Bureau were to provide relief work for both whites and blacks, administer justice for the freedmen and provide for education of freedmen.

The *Abbeville Press* reported on January 24, 1868 that

> *Among the many misfortunes of the poor South is the fact that her little remaining substance is consumed and her people, white and black, plundered by a vast host of swindling adventurers, Bureau agents and officers, who cover the South like locusts.*

Most of the property suffered neglect, particularly farms and plantations. Most menfolk were at war. The women did their best to keep farms in operation, but it was too much. Everything fell into disrepair. Dikes collapsed and many rice fields flooded and were never reclaimed.

Financially, the state and private citizens were heavily invested in Confederate bonds, which became worthless when Lee surrendered. In addition, Union officials seized thousands of bales of cotton that belonged to private citizens. Union agents claimed the cotton had been the property of the Confederate government. The citizens were stunned and shocked by the war, by the deaths of so many of their men and the all-consuming poverty. In the streets of Charleston, rats attacked the weak and feeble, feeding on live homeless, usually widows and children, too weak from hunger and disease to ward the rodents off.

Out of a voting population of 75,000 (white males) South Carolina supplied 71,000 soldiers for the war. Of these, 30,000 died in action or from wounds. No Northern state suffered such a percentage of loss of manpower. Last of all, and most significant, 400,000 slaves in South Carolina were set free. From March to June of 1865, thousands of former slaves deserted the Lowcountry plantations and streamed into Charleston to celebrate their new freedom. Within a few years there were 4,000 more blacks than whites in Charleston, living in filthy, miserable shanties along the waterfront. After the war, there were four million Negroes in the South, mostly uneducated. In South Carolina there were 415,000 Negroes and 290,000 whites. In Charleston County, the ratio of black to white was 2 to 1. There were only nine counties in the state with a white majority, all of them in the upstate.

Union General Robert Scott became the first chief of the Freedmen's Bureau. Some of the work of the Bureau was positive, but much was harmful. A majority of the higher Bureau officials were good men, but most of the subordinate officers and agents were Yankee fanatics or just out-and-out crooks. They arrived from the North under the assumption that the newly freed slaves and their former masters were natural enemies. They often stirred up mischief by giving "the wards of the nation" (freedmen) bad advice, preaching social inequality and arousing hatred between the races.

These men, white and black, many of low character, were called carpetbaggers, and they swarmed like locusts upon the reeling South. They joined forces with white Southern renegades, called scalawags, to form the leadership of the Republican Party for South Carolina.

The Bureau had despotic power in discharging the functions of government and their petty acts aroused the hatred of whites. The Bureau had the authority to arrest and imprison any citizen on the single statement of any Negro. Freedmen were encouraged to believe that the land of their former owners now belonged to them. Bureau agents pushed the idea that every Negro head of family who went to the polls and voted Republican would receive "forty acres and mule." Several Bureau agents sold freedmen red and blue stakes at a dollar per stake, which were to be used in staking off their "forty acres." The agents would then keep the money collected for their own personal use. The idea of "forty acres and mule" became so strong that decades later it was still believed; it caused many freedmen to conclude that they didn't have to work because the government would take care of them.

The main reason Northern agents were sent south was to build up the Republican Party. They quickly organized the Loyal League and began to initiate Negroes into the League. Its chief objective was to keep the white man underfoot. In their printed material, using fear and a small kernel of truth, they taught freedmen that if the Democratic Party ever came back into power, blacks would be put back into slavery.

According to an article in the February 23, 1867 edition of the *New York Times*,

> *We want the southern people well under martial law; we to make sure that all their Negroes have the right to vote. Probably 200,000 will perish this year—blacks and white indiscriminately—mainly in Mississippi, Alabama, Georgia and in the back districts of South Carolina, but there will be a good many left, and it is very important that those who are left should be under martial law. While they are starving, they can be managed more easily. The best way is now we have got them down, to keep them down.*

Whites who challenged the League took the risk of incurring their wrath. The houses and barns of these troublemakers were burned at night. The victim was without redress, as the ruling powers were all against him. For all its initial just and lofty intentions, by 1866 the Freedmen's Bureau was chiefly concerned with propaganda: educating ex-slaves to support the Republican Party.

Congressman Robert Henry commented about the Bureau, "The men who go down there will be your broken-down politicians and your dilapidated preachers; that description of men who are too lazy to work and just a little too honest too steal." White Charlestonians agreed with the former, but not with the latter.

Many of the Northern teachers who arrived in Charleston found they were almost thoroughly despised by whites. "We should none of us be surprised if they make a bonfire of us some dark night."

The Reconstruction Acts unleashed an orgy of corruption and crime in South Carolina. The first elected Republican governor was the former chief of the South Carolina Freedmen's Bureau, Robert K. Scott from Ohio. The wholesale plundering of the state began with Scott's inauguration and continued uninterrupted for eight years.

While serving as governor Scott was seduced by burlesque stripper Pauline Markham. She got him drunk and persuaded the governor to sign fraudulent state bonds over to her and her friends to the tune of $10,000. Scott later moved to Ohio, where he killed a man on Christmas Day 1880 in an argument. The death was ruled accidental homicide.

James K. Pike, a journalist from Maine, wrote a book in 1935, *The Prostrate South*, that remains one of the harshest indictments of Republican Reconstruction. In it he writes,

> *The officials in South Carolina should not be dignified with the name of government. They are men who have studied and practiced the art of legalized theft. They are in no sense different from, or better than, the men who fill the prisons and penitentiaries of the world. They are, in fact…only more daring and audacious. They pick your pockets by law. They rob the poor and rich alike, by law.*

Hiram K. Kimpton of Boston was appointed to the legislature's financial board. Kimpton was a master of juggling figures and dressed in an affected style and elegance. The Charleston *Courier* called him a "smooth article."

John J. Patterson (Honest John) was perhaps the most successful swindler during Reconstruction. In fact, when there was a suggestion that the Republican Party should reform he replied, "Why, there are five more years of good stealing in South Carolina!" His greatest swindle was the manipulation of the Columbia, Greenville and Blue Ridge Railroads. The state spent $6 million and received nothing in return. Some estimates claim that Patterson absconded with more than a third of the money for the railroad venture.

Honest John was elected to the U.S. Senate in 1872. At that time, the state legislature elected U.S. Senators. Patterson claimed the election cost him $40,000 in bribes to each state legislator—bribed by the state's own money, which Honest John had stolen from the railroad swindle.

A Land Commission was established to purchase homes and land for indigent Negroes. The carpetbaggers in charge of the Land Commission confiscated $600,000 for themselves through fraudulent deeds. The sale price on every deed purchased by the state was increased by 15 percent with the extra amount being pocketed by the carpetbagger agent.

One of the sweetest deals (for the agent) was the purchase of eighteen thousand acres in Berkeley County known as Hell Hole Swamp. This land was technically worthless for agricultural purposes, and it cost the state $120,700, or $6.50 per acre. Twenty years later the area was sold for $7,800—$0.40 an acre.

Another opportunity to filch funds was in the furnishing of supplies to members of the legislature. Legislators ordered supplies they needed or wanted for the purpose of conducting state business. The supplies were listed as stationery, sundries, refreshments, furniture, rents and tapestries. In this way, legislators had their private expenses paid for by the State.

By far, the largest expenditures were listed as "refreshments." Members of the legislature ordered wine, liquor, fine cigars, prostitutes and food. During a two-month legislative session, the bill for "refreshments" amounted to $350,000. To have used that much wine and liquor, each member of the legislature must have consumed one gallon of whiskey per day, along with ten bottles of ale and two bottles of wine, and smoked at least a dozen cigars, all paid for by the State. Also listed under "refreshments" were the names of several women.

In the meantime, inmates of the Lunatic Asylum were suffering from lack of food and clothing and the public schools were closed for a time because there were no funds to pay teachers. Convicts were being pardoned from the penitentiary because they could not be fed.

The police and state militia were other means for the Freedmen's Bureau to rule. Under the system there was a chief constable for the state and a deputy constable for each county. John E. Hubbard of New York was appointed chief constable by Governor Scott. Hubbard had a checkered reputation as a brutal policeman in New York City, as did his personal enforcer, James E. Kerrigan, a known gunman for gangsters.

A WORLD TURNED UPSIDE DOWN

Whites, unable to stem the political and social tide against them, withdrew from public life. In March 1867 the U.S. supply ship *Memphis* arrived in Charleston with more than three hundred bushels of corn and other provisions. By the end of the month more than sixteen thousand bushels would arrive in Charleston. The problem of food shortage was magnified by the practice of using corn for whiskey distillation. Upon seeing the devastated condition of their homes and farms, the sight of free Negroes walking the streets and Yankees in charge of their civic affairs, some returning Confederate soldiers stated that they "would rather drink it than eat it."

White Charlestonians were in shock by the change of their lives. Any taxpayer or voter was now eligible to serve on a jury. Judges who refused to seat black jurors were removed from the bench. In all other Southern states, the whites adopted the strategy of electing as many delegates as they could to their constitutional conventions to have some influence on the proceedings.

South Carolina whites had another strategy. The Reconstruction Act required that a majority of registered voters cast their ballots in favor of a constitutional convention. Whites registered in large numbers and then boycotted the election, hoping to prevent the required majority. It failed by a slim margin, mainly because 85 percent of black voters turned out. Native white Carolinians, who had held power for two hundred years, had little say in the writing of the state's new constitution of 1868.

There were 124 delegates to the 1868 Constitutional Convention. Seventy-three were black. Of the fifty-one white delegates, thirty-six were native-born and fifteen were Yankee interlopers. Of the thirty-one members of the Senate, ten were black. In the House, seventy-eight out of 124 were Negroes. Blacks enjoyed the majority in the South Carolina House until 1874. Only twenty-three of the whites were Southern born. The rest were carpetbaggers. The Republican-led legislature from 1868 to 1877 was more famous for its corruption than its accomplishments. There was much buying and selling of votes.

Some of the provisions of the 1868 Constitution included universal male suffrage, the omission of all property qualifications for office, the outlawing of dueling and imprisonment for debt, the legalization of divorce, more legal rights for women, and the opening of schools and state militia to both whites and blacks.

It was a remarkable document bestowing voting rights and educational opportunities "without regard to race or color." However, since the document had been written predominantly by blacks, most white citizens refused to acknowledge it. Many whites had no intention of obeying "a Negro constitution, of a Negro government, establishing Negro equality." The white press called it the "Africanization of South Carolina."

Most whites never accepted the government based on the 1868 Constitution as legitimate. They also began a grass roots, unrelenting campaign against the Reconstruction Regime, black rule and carpetbaggers. During the "People's War" they used propaganda, harassment, intimidation, assault and murder. Most of the Federal troops finally left the state, so law enforcement became the responsibility of the newly elected Republican officials who were helpless in the face of such determined resistance.

In 1869 Chief Constable Hubbard and Governor Scott immediately set about enrolling a state militia to protect blacks. Native whites refused to join, so by the end of the year there were ninety-six thousand Negroes in the militia (90 percent of the Negro voters); 30 percent of the constables were from the North, with the remainder being Negroes. Hubbard armed his constables with Winchester repeating rifles and let them loose. Within two years of the conclusion of the war, the white citizens of South Carolina had to adjust to the shocking fact that the streets and highways were being patrolled by armed Negroes. Truly, their world had turned upside down.

The Ku Klux Klan was established as a secret order to combat what the whites saw as a wholesale assault on their person, property and rights. The members of the Klan saw their organization as an offset to the Freedmen's Bureau. Whatever the original intentions of the Klan, the organization was soon taken over by a lower class of men, who began to lynch, whip and punish Negroes as well as the more corrupt carpetbaggers and scalawags. The men in the Klan discovered that the disguise of their robes afforded them protection from their crimes, so as time went on, they became bolder in their acts of violence. A persistent myth in the South is that the KKK was formed to protect whites from the black militia. In truth the KKK appeared well before the militia.

Emancipation had stripped the white elite of their human and physical property. In South Carolina, former slaves and blacks made up a majority of the electorate in 1867. During Reconstruction the black militia who patrolled the streets and highways to keep peace never forgot that the essence of slavery had been physical domination. Unfortunately, most black men had no military experience, while almost every white man had substantial military experience.

Black voters may have frightened white men, but the black militia terrified them. Most whites considered black men to be inherently unfit for citizenship and as blacks assumed the roles of statesmen, whites portrayed them as ignorant and comical; a mob. When Republicans and Yankees took over South Carolina, it seemed to whites that a mob had taken over the state.

The Ku Klux Klan was the first major offensive by the whites against Republican Reconstruction. From 1868–71, the KKK ran rampant through the state. Once the United States government took control of South Carolina, Klan violence was muted, mainly due to the increased amount of regular army. However, the white elite planters also had to deal with the renegade whites who sided with Republicans and Yankees. The Klan burned the buildings and crops of white race-traitors who "refused to unite with others in the recent proscriptions against colored people." Nightriders targeted white men who were "in league" with Republican Reconstructionists.

James Henry Hammond, a South Carolina planter, noted in 1845:

> There were no mobs in the slave South, only the "habitual vigilance, concerned in the maintenance of order." The people might assemble to chastise an abolitionist, but this was "no more of a mob, than a rally of shepherds to chase a wolf out of their pastures would be one." The planters believed if abolition were forced upon them, society would collapse—former slaves would plunder the land.

Governor Scott sent a message to General Wade Hampton that if he did not speak out against the Klan violence, a long-feared race war may erupt. Hampton, former Confederate general, may have been the most popular and powerful white native South Carolinian at the time. Hampton responded to the governor's appeal with an address that was carried in every South Carolina newspaper asking for the "preservation of order." Almost immediately, the attacks ceased. The Republican governor got the peace he sought, but the incident also demonstrated where the real power was: with Wade Hampton and the white community.

In 1872, F.J. Moses was elected Republican governor. Formerly Speaker of the House, Moses was considered a degenerate even though he was from a well-respected family. He began his political life in support of secession. He was secretary to South Carolina Governor Pickens during the war and was known across South Carolina as the man who "tore down the American flag at Fort Sumter." During Reconstruction Moses was derisively called "King of the Scalawags" by whites, but soon picked up another nickname: "the Robber Governor."

He was elected to office with very little personal money. His salary as governor was $3,400 and when he left office his assets totaled $225,000. He sold everything connected to his office: pardons, military titles, honors, seats in Congress and state building contracts. Moses pardoned 457 convicts during his two years in office.

Moses was indicted for fraud and bribery along with 124 members of his legislature, but none ever were brought to trial. Charges were slowly dropped as Moses bribed or intimidated the legal officials who were investigating him. He handed out tracts of land, confiscated businesses and cash, lots of cash. After his term as governor, Moses moved to New York where he became a swindler. He was convicted of fraud in New York and spent more than a year in prison.

James K. Pike wrote in *The Prostrate South:*

> *The last administration (Scott) stole right and left...the whole of the administration was a mass of rottenness, and the present administration (Moses) is born of that corruption. They plunder and they glory in it. They steal and defy you to prove it. The Treasure of the State has been so thoroughly plundered there is nothing left to steal.*

Wade Hampton commented that it was time for white Southerners to "dedicate themselves to the redemption of the South." For "self defense," rifle clubs formed in Charleston; the first was called the Carolina Rifle Club. It was another response by whites to the Negro majority militia. The members would meet weekly for drilling. They would conduct shooting matches and parades. During a municipal election in Charleston, a riot occurred on the streets and Republican authorities were forced to call on the Carolina Rifle Club to help maintain law.

Rifle clubs were established in other Carolina communities; sometimes they were called "saber clubs." These clubs were soon to play an enormous part in South Carolina politics as the basis of the Democratic campaign for governor by Wade Hampton.

MASSACRES AND THE ELECTION OF 1876

The turning point in the war against Reconstruction in South Carolina came on the nation's one-hundredth birthday. On July 4, 1876, a black militia unit drilled in the streets of Hamburg, a town on the Savannah River. Hamburg was the home of former Confederate officer Matthew Butler and his white rifle club. However, the town's populace was almost entirely black and most town officials were black. The city's justice of the peace was a former slave and Union army veteran, Prince Rivers, a major general in the militia. Hamburg was considered a symbol of black independence.

There was a face-off in the street between the black militia and two young white planters, Thomas Butler and Henry Getzen. The young planters demanded right of way on the street for their buggy. After trading insults and threats, the black militia finally gave way. Warrants were sworn out against each other. Justice Prince Rivers set the hearing for July 8.

On the appointed day, Butler and Getzen arrived with their counsel, Matthew Butler (no relation), and a host of armed white men from surrounding counties, wearing red shirts. Fearing for their lives, the black militiamen barricaded themselves in their drill room. The Red Shirts surrounded the drill room and demanded the militia surrender. Shots were fired from the drill room and a white man was killed. A cannon was brought in to demolish the walls of the building. Black militiamen tried to flee, but most were caught and taken prisoner. After a heated discussion, the Red Shirt leaders identified six of the black militia leaders and executed them with a bullet to the head. The Red Shirts then told the rest of the Republicans to run and fired on them as they fled.

This massacre landed most of the participants in jail and brought national attention to the incident. More Federal troops were sent to South Carolina. Francis Dawson of the *News and Courier* called the Hamburg event "barbarous in the extreme" and "a wholly unjustifiable affray."

Butler organized a boycott of the paper and challenged Dawson to a duel. Dawson was adamantly opposed to dueling and refused to acknowledge Butler's challenge. Dawson opposed dueling on moral and religious grounds. Throughout his career as a newspaper owner and editor, Dawson fought against men of violence and their traditions, especially dueling and lynching. And on August 10, 1876, his commitment to those views against violence was pushed to the limit.

Colonel Robert Barnwell Rhett, editor of *Charleston Journal*, published a scathing denunciation of Dawson, calling him an "ingrate, liar and coward." The next day Dawson responded by alluding to a Louisiana duel in which Rhett had killed Judge Cooley. Dawson claimed Rhett had been brought to South Carolina as a professional killer.

Rhett was a man who believed in acting strictly to the codes of dueling (covered in *Wicked Charleston: The Dark Side of the Holy City*, Chapter Six), which provided that if someone called you a liar you were expected to hit, shoot or challenge by presence. Rhett, having given the insult, had nothing more to do under the code, except to put himself in the position to be challenged. He did so for two days in succession.

At noon on August 11, 1876, Rhett stepped from his office on East Bay Street and strolled up Broad toward Meeting. That was the hour when Dawson usually went to his office on Broad Street. Rhett was followed by Frank McHugh and Alfred Williams. All men were armed. Williams was armed with a .28-caliber six shooter. In Virginia, Williams's home state, the .28 six-shooter was regarded as a formidable weapon. The first time Williams showed it to someone in Charleston he was told, "Sonny, if you shoot any gentleman in Charleston with that thing…he'll take it from you and beat you with it for insultin' him." In Charleston, the smallest caliber that was tolerated was a .38. The really well-dressed man wore a .44. A man without a revolver felt undressed and embarrassed; it was as much a part of a gentleman's attire as were trousers and a hat.

The doors of the shops on Broad Street and the steps of the post office and city hall were crowded with men anxious to see a fight. Mayor Cunningham had posted policemen along the sidewalks in anticipation of trouble. Dawson walked down the south side of Broad Street with his brother-in-law, Jimmy Morgan. Rhett and his party strolled on the north side of Broad. To the disappointment of the onlookers, nothing happened. Dawson refused to respond to Rhett as they passed on the street. Rhett, having put himself in the position to be challenged, felt vindicated. Dawson, Rhett concluded, was a coward for not calling him out.

The Hamburg massacre galvanized the white community of South Carolina. If there was to be any stability in their government, they believed they had to take control from the Yankee interlopers and the freedmen. Red Shirt units were organized throughout the state. Mounted and armed Red Shirts arrived at Republican rallies and demanded their opponents "divide time" with them. The presence of the Red Shirts (Democrats) transformed a peaceful political meeting into a riot. Red Shirt leaders urged the assassination of Republican officials. Dozens of black militiamen were killed; more Federal troops arrived in South Carolina.

The Democrats considered the Reconstruction government a slave revolt, a challenge to the traditional white authority. The Republicans, duly elected, considered the Red Shirts and the Klan as threats to the legal government. The federal government considered the state to be just short of open rebellion.

The Port Royal *Standard and Commercial* of October 5, 1876, wrote in an editorial: "The entire Democratic party of the State is fully armed and organized...more dependence is placed in the shotgun than argument."

The Democrats needed a man who could break the hold the Republicans had on state government. Wade Hampton was the man.

Born March 28, 1818, on Hasell Street in Charleston, Hampton was a former Confederate general and the grandson of a celebrated Revolutionary hero. Before the War Between the States, Hampton had been one of the richest men in the south, and after the war he might have been the most loved man in the state, by whites and blacks. He had treated his former slaves fairly in the aftermath of the war, helping them adjust to their new life of freedom. He was not against the Negro, but against the powers of Washington. Hampton advocated "force without violence."

Large groups of Democrats roamed the state in support and defense of Hampton, wearing red shirts and armed with pistols and shotguns. The rifle clubs became the organizations that helped propel Hampton to victory. He toured the state, accompanied by hundreds of mounted white men clad in red shirts. At one stop, he encountered a woman lying on the ground with a sash identifying her as "South Carolina." He dismounted and picked her up. The symbolism was simple: Wade Hampton was the savior to raise the state up from the shackles of Yankee rule.

The Charleston Light Dragoons, also called the Hampton Mounted Social Club, patrolled the city at night during the 1876 campaign. On September 6, black Democrats supporting Hampton held a political rally in Archer's Hall at the corner of George and King Streets. A mob of black Republicans attacked the black Democrats and their white escorts near Citadel Green (Marion Square). Shots were fired and a riot erupted. Two reporters for the *News and Courier* were beaten. While on horseback, editor Dawson was attacked at the corner of King and Clifford Streets, but managed to escape with little injury. The driver of a horse-drawn streetcar was attacked at 11:00 p.m. The driver, Edward Salters, was dragged from his car and beaten. He was saved by a policeman, Sergeant John Malone, but the two were pursued by the mob to Malone's house where they barricaded themselves. The house was pelted with cobblestones and brickbats. Many white men were arrested just to save them from the mob.

On his way home, Alfred Williams (he of the infamous .28-caliber six shooter) was set upon by a band of fifteen blacks at the corner of Hasell and King. Shots were exchanged and Williams then realized how ineffective his puny six-shooter was, and why it was considered a worthless gun in Charleston. After a moment the blacks stopped firing, laughed and walked away. Williams said it was "humiliating to be routed by the foe, yet worse to be the subject of merriment." Williams never knew if they were laughing "at me or my revolver, or both."

For several days blacks roamed upper King Street "from midnight until sunrise breaking windows, robbing stores and attacking every white man who showed his face." Before order was restored, one hundred people were hurt, one black and one white were killed. For the next several months twenty local rifle clubs patrolled the streets; sometimes there were more than five hundred men patrolling the streets at night. South Carolina became the foremost issue in the national campaign. Republicans tried to portray Southern Democrats as ruthless savages preying on helpless people.

On Monday, October 16, 1876, a massacre took place at the Brick Church in Cainhoy. During a Democratic meeting in the country, blacks began shooting from ruined houses and behind oaks at the assembled Democrats. Most of the white men were unarmed and those who were armed had nothing more powerful than pistols. Five whites and one black were killed, and twenty more were wounded. Most of the dead had been mutilated and some of the wounded were not found until the next day, also maimed and mutilated and left to die.

During the Chamberlain-Hampton campaign of 1876, there were a total of fifty-five deaths and more than one hundred injured during the following riots and armed confrontations.

Hamburg: July 8, 1876 (eight dead: seven blacks, one white)

Charleston: September 6, 1876 (two dead: one black, one white, and one hundred injured)

Ellenton: September 16–18 (forty-two dead: two whites, forty blacks)

Cainhoy: October 16 (five whites dead, a dozen injured)

A WORLD TURNED UPSIDE DOWN

It is impossible to know what the outcome would have been with a fair and free election. The Democrats cheated and intimidated, bribed and threatened, and the Republicans did likewise. The election laws had been designed by Reconstruction Republicans to facilitate fraud, and the Democrats beat them at their own game. Martin Gary urged Democrats to "vote early and often." Hundreds of men crossed from Georgia and North Carolina to vote for Hampton again and again. Thousands of white underage boys voted. Many poll managers were bribed, and others who were already sympathetic needed no inducement. They administered the voting oath to underage boys: "I do solemnly swear that I am not twenty-one years of age and am not entitled lawfully to vote at this election." The "nots" were whispered so that bystanders could not hear. Troops of Red Shirts rode about from poll to poll voting at each, hindering and scattering Negroes who were trying to do likewise.

On Election Day there were problems in Charleston. At 3:00 p.m. at the corner of Meeting and Broad Streets, E.W.M. Mackey was reading election news to a large crowd of Negroes. He finished and walked into the *News and Courier* offices on Broad Street. He got into a discussion with several inebriated white men who were watching the *Courier*'s election bulletin board. As they discussed the election, one of the men struck Mackey in the face; there was a scuffle and one shot was fired from a small French derringer. Negroes on the street rushed to the intersection of Meeting and Broad and shouted that Mackey had been killed. Less than five minutes later a mob of fifty Negroes was charging down Broad Street. The white men fired guns from the south side of Broad. The Negroes retreated to the north side, past city hall. The police dispersed the crowd quickly and some of the black police went inside the Guard House and came out carrying Winchester rifles. They opened fire on the whites in the street.

The first victims were George E. Walter, a local businessman, and his son Endicott. They were returning from dinner to their office on Adger's Wharf, walking on the north side of Broad in front of the courthouse. Endicott was killed and his father severely wounded. Dr. Cassimer Patrick, standing next to a column of St. Michael's church, was also shot. Soon more than one thousand Negroes were in the street, carrying sticks and clubs. They stormed the front doors of the Guard House, shouting, "Give us the guns!"

Members of the rifle clubs were scattered about the city, most of them at their stores and offices at work. The police sent word to Citadel Green, where U.S. troops were quartered. By 5:30 p.m. five hundred rifle club men had assembled and organized together with the U.S. Army. The city was subdued four hours after the riot began. The next day, all stores were closed and schools were suspended. Rifle club members and the U.S. Army had every intersection guarded. The casualty total of this riot included one killed, twenty-two men shot or beaten, including two policemen as well as Francis Dawson, who was shot through his calf as he rode through the mob.

The riot delayed the election returns in Charleston. On November 10, 1876, the final tally came in: Hampton (D): 92,261; Chamberlain (R): 91,127. It appeared that Hampton had defeated Chamberlain by less than 1,200 votes, but each party claimed victory, accusing the other of fraud. National newspapers covered the daily drama on their front pages. Within a week of the election, the attention of the country had shifted to the South Carolina State House and the battle between the divided House, Senate and the two governors.

The Democrats claimed 65 of 124 members of the House. They organized, and in an effort to avoid bloodshed, they left the statehouse and assembled in Carolina Hall. Sixty-five was the majority and guaranteed the Democrats a quorum, so they legally made up the South Carolina House.

The Republicans, with 59 of 116 members in the Senate, claimed a quorum and assembled in the State House. On November 30, the Democratic House moved back to the State House. Both parties claimed victory and refused to give up. For four days Democrats and Republicans ate and slept in the legislative chamber, with each group trying to conduct regular legislative business.

Outside, friends of both parties gathered in large numbers, with police, militia and military trying to keep the crowd from turning into a mob. On December 6, Chamberlain, supported by Federal troops, was inaugurated governor. Hampton addressed the people claiming that "the people of South Carolina have elected me Governor, and by the Eternal God, I will be Governor."

For the next four months, South Carolina had rival houses and governors, each claiming to be the legitimate government. Since it takes money to run government, white taxpayers refused to pay their taxes. However, at Hampton's request, they voluntarily contributed 10 percent of their tax liability to his (Democrat) government. Any state agency that wanted to operate had to go to the Hampton government for funds. That began a trickling of defections from the Republican government, which existed only because of the life support from Federal troops. After Rutherford B. Hayes was inaugurated president, both Hampton and Chamberlain visited Hayes, who stated, "The whole army of the United States would be inadequate to enforce the authority of Governor Chamberlain." Hayes ordered the evacuation of Federal troops from South Carolina and on April 3, 1877, the troops began to leave. One week later Chamberlain and the Republicans vacated their offices in the State House. Wade Hampton, the white Democrats and former Confederates once again controlled South Carolina.

The Democrats slashed public spending, reduced police and fire departments and canceled programs for capital improvements. Charleston was a shabby city in the 1880s with unpaved streets, open sewers and polluted drinking water. There was no central water or sewer system. More than seven thousand privies leaked one hundred thousand pounds of human waste a day and contaminated private wells. The city and its business community was dominated by the same men who had been in charge in 1860: older men who rejected those new Yankee ideas. Younger men with the new outlook were not welcomed into the political and economic fold. The old relaxed style was entrenched: go to work at 10:30 a.m., dinner at 3:00 p.m. and then back to the office to close up. The old style of noncompetitive business wheeling and dealing returned. Unlike most cities in the South, Charleston looked behind, not ahead.

In 1878, Hampton ran unopposed for governor. Hampton did his best to be governor of all people by appointing blacks and Republicans to his governmental posts. Many blacks were still elected to public office. During the Hampton era, there was equal funding for black and white schools, but despite those efforts, 78.5 percent of blacks and 22 percent of whites were totally illiterate in 1880.

Segregation was strongest in churches. Whereas blacks had formerly worshipped in the same churches with whites (albeit in the balcony or back rows), blacks left the white churches and formed their own congregations. First among the black churches was the African Methodist Episcopal. By 1885, 91 percent of South Carolinians were either Baptist or Methodist.

In 1882, the "Eight Box Law," written by Charlestonian Edward McCrady Jr., was passed by the state assembly. The law got its name from the requirement that there be eight separate ballot boxes for different offices (a voter had to be able to read to know where to place his ballot). Another provision in the law was that every voter must reregister before June 1, or be forever banned from voting. Within four years, tens of thousands of blacks in South Carolina were disenfranchised. Voting districts were redrawn, leaving only one black majority district. The state's last nineteenth-century black congressman was defeated for reelection in 1896.

Francis W. Dawson's *News and Courier* was considered part of the New South. Dawson recommended that Charlestonians let the past be past and work toward building a new South Carolina. If a newspaper's importance is reflected by how the community responds, the *Courier* had no effect on Charleston. Charleston completely rejected the notion of the New South. Dawson suggested that Charleston needed "about five hundred Yankees of the right stripe to put a new face on affairs and make the whole place throb with life and vivid force." Imagine how that was received by the white elites. For most whites in the state, Reconstruction ruined the Republican Party in South Carolina for several generations.

Charleston was the largest city in South Carolina but its importance had been in decline since the early nineteenth century. In 1800, Charleston was the fourth largest city in the United States, but by 1890 it had fallen to sixty-eighth. Within the South, it had dropped from the largest to sixth during the same time period. There were many reasons, one of which was the advent of steamships. During the age of sail Charleston was on the main trading route. Once ships could steam against the currents and wind, Charleston was no longer a prime destination. Northern railroads also began to siphon traffic off to New York and Philadelphia.

And then, on August 25, 1885, a massive hurricane hit the city (125 mile per hour winds with a large tidal surge). Twenty-one people were killed and 90 percent of homes were damaged, with damages totaling more than $2 million ($31 million in 2000 money). One year later, August 31, 1886, the city was rocked by a major earthquake that would have registered higher than a 7.0 on the Richter scale. More than two thousand buildings were destroyed with three thousand more damaged. One hundred and ten people died of injuries and subsequent disease. Property damage in the city reached more than $6 million (equal to $96.4 million).

In a short twenty-five years, Charleston had endured the longest modern military bombardment, which had destroyed millions of dollars in property and infrastructure. Also, a Federal blockade of the harbor had stifled and squeezed the economy into shambles, and the loss of the war had cost the state most of its assets (of which slavery was a large part). Then, the city endured the plundering of the state's treasury by corrupt Federal and local officials (carpetbaggers and scalawags). And now, two major disasters pummeled the city within a year. A grand dame, Charleston wore its shabby cloak of ruin with pride. As other cities of the old Confederacy embraced the New South, Charleston did not. Daughters of the old elite were happy to earn $4.22 for a six-day workweek in a shop on King Street. Their daily wages ($0.70) were barely above what their grandfathers had paid to maintain a slave field hand. During this time, family came to matter more than money.

THE MURDER OF CAPTAIN DAWSON

Austin John Reeks was born in London on May 17, 1840. The Reeks were one of the oldest Catholic families in England that traced its history back to the War of the Roses. The family had never recanted its religious affiliation during the persecutions by Henry VIII and Elizabeth, even after several Reeks had been burned at the stake.

Unfortunately, the family fortune was decimated by bad decisions during the 1840s, and the future for young Austin John's education did not look positive. However, a sister of Mrs. Reeks had inherited a considerable estate when her husband, William A. Dawson, died. The aunt intended Austin John to be the beneficiary of her wealth, but she died without a will. Other members of the family were able to claim the estate through legal maneuvers. That left Austin John, at age eighteen, without an education or vocation and little means of acquiring either, other than using his excellent tenor voice to pursue a career in the theatre. This brought much displeasure to his family. People in the theatre were considered to be lowlifes, drunkards and irresponsible.

In London, as he made the rounds of theatrical companies, Austin John spent many hours writing plays. One particular manuscript reveals much about the man that Austin John was to become and sheds light on his later life in Charleston. Titled *Never Judge by Appearances*, it was a simple, highly moralistic work that placed the heroine in a position in which she was torn between her "duty" to her boring husband and her desire for a more romantic man, a scoundrel who only wants to take her virtue. By the end, she has realized the error of her ways and confesses her secret desire and sins to her husband, who forgives her.

The tension in the Reeks family was fierce, due to the lack of money, their loss of social standing and Austin's intention to pursue a career in the theatre. Austin searched about for a way out of his dead-end life and a path away from his family. Imagine their surprise when he announced in the autumn of 1861 that he was sailing to America to fight for the Confederate States! He later wrote that he "had a sincere sympathy with the Southern people in their struggle for independence and felt it would be a pleasant thing to help them secure their freedom." He had contacted the captain of a Confederate steamer, the *Nashville*, docked at Southampton, about signing on as a deckhand. His family was horrified because they thought it would dishonor the family name even more than being in the theatre. They feared he would be hanged as a pirate on the passage across the ocean. Austin John told them he was leaving to be "hanged under a name of my own."

As his first name he chose Francis, the name of his patron saint, Francis of Assisi. His middle name was to be Warrington, the name of a family friend. The surname he chose was Dawson, after his dead uncle whose money would have given Austin the higher education.

Thus, it was a twenty-year-old Francis Warrington Dawson who left Southampton on February 2, 1862, on the *Nashville*, and once on the open seas, was mustered into the service of the Confederate States of America Navy. Upon his arrival in America, he soon found navy life too dull. After all, he had crossed the ocean to get into a fight. He secured his release from the navy and joined the Purcell Battery in Richmond as a private. By August 1862 he had been promoted to first lieutenant and by April 1864 he was a captain. He saw action at Mechanicsville, Second Manassas, Fredericksburg, Gettysburg, Chattanooga, Knoxville, Spotsylvania and he was wounded at Five Forks in 1865.

After the war, Dawson worked at the Richmond *Examiner* for several years before moving to Charleston to assume the position of assistant editor of the Charleston *Mercury*. The *Mercury* and its owner/editor, Robert Barnwell Rhett, had been a leading proponent of secession. In fact, the *Mercury* made international headlines on the night of December 20, 1860, when it had a newspaper on the streets fifteen minutes after South Carolina had seceded from the Union. However, the *Mercury* was struggling to stay in print and Dawson realized the paper was going to fold sooner rather than later.

Three months after his arrival in Charleston, Dawson married Virginia Fourgeaud, the eldest but sickly daughter of a prominent French Catholic family. Dawson threw himself into his work and, using the Fourgeaud family as a foundation, he began to make social and business contacts in

Charleston. By 1867, Dawson had purchased one-third interest in the ailing Charleston *News* and worked feverously to boost circulation. The *Mercury* soon closed down, leaving only two papers in Charleston, the *News* and the *Courier*, the oldest paper in the South.

Dawson lost his wife to consumption in 1872, and one year later, he and his financial partners succeeded in purchasing the *Courier*. On April 7, 1873, the first edition of the Charleston *News and Courier* hit the streets. Nine months later, Dawson married again, this time to Sarah Ida Fowler Morgan.

Dawson was not "born Charleston" as the expression goes. He was an outsider who became an insider, as much of an insider as someone not born in the city can ever be. He gained his influence by hard work, intelligence and personality. The fact that he was an outsider who had fought for the Confederacy—and had even been injured and captured by the Yankees—did much to make him acceptable. Most of his editorial positions were also most likely to be in line with most of the white elite, such as his condescending attitude that whites should act as guardians of the less fortunate race, an opinion that did not make Dawson loved by the black community. However, he did have his strong opinions that sometimes ruffled the whites as well.

By the 1880s Dawson was considered one of the most powerful men in South Carolina. The *News and Courier* had statewide daily delivery and was the most influential paper in the South. Dawson, having no ambition for public office, was content to play his powerful role behind the scenes and on the pages of the paper. The *New York Times* called Dawson "a man whose head was cool on all occasions" and who molded political fortunes with a "merciless application of the party whip."

Dawson considered the chief evils in Charleston to be whiskey, gambling and pistols. Of these three sins, pistols were the worst, but nothing, except lynching, was more embarrassing to Dawson than the Code Duello. Before the war, dueling had been a symbol of aristocratic integrity, but after the war, it lost much of its romantic flavor. After the tremendous loss of life and the tragedy of watching maimed Confederate veterans try to pick up the pieces of their shattered lives, the romance of dueling was gone. Dawson was vocal and strident in his opposition of dueling and the carrying of concealed weapons.

Dawson began a battle against dueling, lynching and hip pocket justice even though, in various duels, he had served as a "best friend" or second, for Henry Rivers Pollard, editor and publisher of the Richmond *Examiner*. Dawson's anti-dueling editorial campaign culminated with the passage of a tough anti-dueling law by the General Assembly. For his anti-dueling efforts Dawson was knighted by Pope Leo XIII, making him the only American newspaper editor ever so honored.

By 1888, Dawson was so powerful that his endorsement of George Bryan as Charleston mayor was almost enough to ensure his election. Bryan helped break the hold that Governor (and later Senator) Ben Tillman had on the city government. Even though he was at the pinnacle of his influence, Dawson's business was failing. Despite its position as the paper of the state, the *News and Courier* was having severe financial problems. Dawson had gone to New York for funding. He had attempted to purchase a good life insurance policy on himself for his wife and his children. However, Dawson was not as good a risk as he hoped. His health had not been good for several years. He lived a life of stress and had little time for exercise and recreation. He also was suffering from a painful ulcer. He returned in February 1889 firm in his position as the "colossus of Broad Street" and with the hope that his financial problems were behind him.

However, on Tuesday, March 12, 1889, everything came to a violent, ironic end.

One week before, Dawson had called Police Chief Joseph Golden to the editor's office. Dawson told Golden about an anonymous report which alleged that Dawson's Swiss governess had been seen in disreputable company, namely in the company of a married gentleman, Dr. Thomas McDow. McDow lived at the corner of Rutledge and Bull Streets, less then half a block from Dawson's Bull Street dwelling. In fact, the two properties backed up against each other. McDow's piazza had a good view of Dawson's back yard. Concerned about the welfare of the young woman, his charge, and of the influence the woman had over his children, Dawson asked Golden to assign a detective to investigate the matter. Later that day, Golden assigned Sergeant John Dunn to the task.

The following Monday afternoon, Dunn followed the governess, Helene Marie Burdayron. Dunn noted that she showed no unusual behavior but she did "attract a great deal of attention on account of her dress." Miss Burdayron was a beautiful twenty-two year old woman from Switzerland, and her attire was of the European standard rather than the more conservative Charleston Victorian-era style. She cut quite a figure in her fashionable snug-fitting dress and wide-brimmed hat with white feathers. She was the type of woman that set tongues to wagging; a beautiful, mysterious stranger.

A WORLD TURNED UPSIDE DOWN

Dunn followed Helene as she took the red car trolley at Meeting Street near Broad. Dr. McDow boarded the trolley at Wentworth Street and the two rode together to the upper terminal where they both exited and strolled about the sparsely populated streets. He lost sight of them for a while but saw them standing in front of a Negro shanty. He reported he could not determine if they were exiting the house or not. Later Dunn reported that McDow returned to his house without the woman. Dunn wrote his report and turned it over to his chief.

The next morning Chief Golden reported all this to Dawson, who carefully read Dunn's report. Dawson told the chief that he would attend to the matter on his way home that evening. Golden told Dawson not to take any direct action; McDow's reputation was not the best, and it would be better if Dawson ignored the man. Golden was so concerned that Dawson would do something rash that he stationed extra police in Dawson's neighborhood that afternoon.

Shortly after three o'clock, earlier than usual, Dawson headed for home. In his coat pocket was Sergeant Dunn's report. Dawson rode the blue trolley to the corner of Bull Street and stepped off the car, waving goodbye to several friends. Instead of going home, Dawson walked to McDow's residence at 101 Rutledge, tapping his cane along the sidewalk. The doctor's office was on the bottom floor of the house and opened from the Rutledge Street side. Dawson pulled the leather strap that rang the doorbell.

A few hours later, Sarah Dawson received a call from the *News and Courier* office inquiring about the whereabouts of her husband. She told the caller that her husband was not home, and was told in return that Mr. Dawson had left the office more than two hours before and that police were looking for him. She then became anxious. A few moments later she received a knock on her door. She opened the door to a slightly built man with dark complexion and dark hair. Upon her opening the door, he became nervous and agitated. Sarah asked what he wanted. He replied "nothing" and left, almost running down the sidewalk.

Less than half an hour later Henry Baynard arrived at the Dawson house pale and trembling. Baynard was a member of the *News and Courier* staff and for a moment Sarah believed that her husband might have killed Baynard's brother. Swinton Baynard had recently just quit the *Courier* and taken a position at the rival *World*. Swinton had departed on bitter terms. Dawson considered him a traitor and several times he had stated that Swinton "deserved death." However, a few minutes later, Major

Hemphill, the assistant editor of the *Courier* arrived and Sarah asked him flat out, "Is my husband dead?"

Mayor Bryan was presiding over a city council meeting that evening when a messenger appeared in City Hall chambers and asked to speak privately to the mayor. Bryan returned a moment later, his face ashen. He announced, "Gentlemen...a great public calamity has come to us; Captain F.W. Dawson now lies dead in this city." The mayor sank into his seat and began to sob.

The next day, the front page of the *News and Courier* was devoted to the death and murder of their editor and owner.

CAPTAIN DAWSON MURDERED
KILLED IN THE AFTERNOON IN THE OFFICE
OF DR. MCDOW
MCDOW ARRESTED FOR MURDER

The funeral was held in front of an overflowing crowd and the procession slowly made its way down King Street. Almost every shop and store was closed and draped with black bunting; the streets were lined with thousands of citizens to pay their respects to their adopted son. But almost as soon as the day of mourning passed, everyone's attention was drawn to the events of the investigation. It soon became the only topic of conversation among gentlemen during their business lunches and among ladies during their tea parties. This was the chain of events, as most people understood them:

Dawson had arrived to confront McDow about his improper dalliance with Miss Burdayron. The two men had argued. A black carriage driver named Harper was waiting for his party up the street and heard two men shouting. He then heard a muted gunshot. He heard one man shout, "You would take my life and now I have taken yours!" Immediately afterward, Harper watched a gentleman close the windows of McDow's basement and a moment later he noticed McDow standing on his piazza as "cool as a cucumber." Harper watched McDow's butler hook up the McDow carriage, and several minutes later, McDow hustled his wife and daughter out of the house and into the carriage with the butler driving them away. McDow then went back inside the house. Three hours later, McDow had turned himself in to the police and confessed to the murder of Francis Dawson.

A WORLD TURNED UPSIDE DOWN

Details from the inquest that contradicted the known story set the gossip and speculation into overdrive. McDow had initially told the police that Dawson had attacked him with his cane. The two men struggled and McDow was able to grab a pistol and shoot the editor in self-defense. However, the inquest revealed no wounds on the doctor from the caning, and more damning, the gunshot wound indicated that Dawson had been shot in the back. The investigators also discovered something more grim and sinister. McDow had dumped Dawson's hat and cane in the privy, pulled up floorboards in the basement and dug a shallow grave. Dawson's body had been dumped in the grave, but evidently the floorboards could not be replaced, so McDow dragged the body back out, filled in the dirt and replaced the boards. Only then did he contact the police.

The public was titillated by other rumors swirling around the story. One rumor was that the *Courier* had been investigating a story about false death certificates in the black community. In an attempt to defraud insurance companies, McDow was signing fraudulent death certificates for a portion of the insurance settlement. Another story rumored that Dawson himself was having an affair with Miss Burdayron and the two men fought over their romantic intentions.

No one doubted the outcome of the trial. The *Courier* pulled out all stops in their attempt to illustrate as much of McDow's bad character as they could discover. They reported that McDow had been involved in a shooting in Mississippi before he arrived in Charleston. They also reported his alleged drug use and his reputation as an abortionist. His marriage to a rather plain and plump German woman was suggested to have been an arranged affair for money.

When the case was called to court on June 24, 1889, the largest crowd ever to assemble at the courthouse crammed into the chambers. Hundreds gathered on the sidewalks. Reporters from New York, Boston, Philadelphia and Chicago were in town to cover the trial. It was a mixed jury, seven blacks and five whites, one of the first times since Reconstruction that a jury had a majority of blacks in a murder trial.

On the first day of the trial, the first important witness was Dr William Middleton Michel, the man who performed the autopsy on Dawson. Dr. Michel testified that Dawson had been shot in the back and that no powder burns were on Dawson's clothes, indicating that the gun had not been fired at close range.

On the second day of trial, Miss Burdayron took the stand. The prosecutor asked her age.

"Twenty-two," she said.

She stated that from their first meeting, Dr. McDow had urged her to run away with him. She also said that McDow had visited her secretly at the Dawson's home, and she had accepted gifts from him, including a gold watch and several books.

"Has Dr. McDow ever kissed you?" the prosecutor asked.

"Yes."

"How many times?"

"Many times."

The lawyer held up a novel, *Twixt Love and Law*, a sensational Victorian tale about a married man's passion for a single girl. He asked her about the book and Helene said it had been a gift from Dr. McDow.

"Do you understand that the story in the book reflects your relationship with the doctor?" the lawyer asked.

"No, no," said Helene. "In the book, a single girl loves a married man. It was not the case for me. I love him not!"

The defense tried to muddle the scientific claims that Dawson had been shot in the back and used the testimony of the carriage driver, Harper, to support McDow's claim of self-defense. The doctor's lawyers also mentioned that the police were so concerned about Dawson's violent intention toward McDow that extra officers were in the neighborhood to protect the editor in case he got into trouble. Ex-Mayor Sayle was also called to testify and he described Dawson as "more on the bulldog order than anything else I can think of." They argued hard on the self-defense angle, traditionally an easy route to acquittal in South Carolina. They went so far as to pull out the old "a man's home is his castle" argument, and a man's right to defend himself while under violent attack in his home.

The jury retired for deliberations just after lunch on Saturday, June 29, and less than three hours later they returned with a verdict of "not guilty." The large crowd erupted into a cheer. It took the judge several moments to restore order. McDow exited the courthouse and a large crowd of Negroes in the street cheered as his carriage pulled away.

That reaction strengthened the suspicions of Dawson's friends that the black majority jury had been sympathetic toward McDow from the beginning. One of Dawson's friends, Solicitor Julien Jervey, declared that it was "the first time on record that a white man had been tried by a jury on which there were colored men in any trial of note."

McDow was barred by the medical community but he continued to practice medicine in the black community. His wife and daughter left him after the trial, and McDow died alone in his house in July 1904. His body was not discovered until four days later, due to the foul odor emitting from the house on Rutledge Street.

Francis Dawson, English Confederate, the colossus of Broad Street, who waged a battle against dueling, lynching and hip pocket justice died in a most ironic manner: killed in a fight by a concealed weapon. In the end, even Dawson's knighthood by the pope for his stand against violence could not save his life.

CHAPTER THREE

RAISING HELL ON CHICCO STREET

The Charleston *Courier* complained that Prohibition ruined everyone's taste for fine liquor. Because they could no longer obtain brandy and Madeira, they guzzled "Hell Hole (Swamp) corn likker."

PROHIBITION — WRINGING, SOPPING WET

Author's note: The Eighteenth Amendment to the Constitution was passed by Congress in 1917. It was ratified by three-quarters of the states by 1919 and prohibited the manufacture or sale of alcoholic beverages within the boundaries of the United States. The Volstead Act of 1919, also known as the National Prohibition Enforcement Act, gave the Eighteenth Amendment some teeth. It clearly defined an alcoholic beverage as one with an alcoholic content greater than 0.5 percent.

When the Volstead Act was passed, Charleston was dragged kicking and screaming into Prohibition. Many citizens simply ignored the law. However, leading up to national Prohibition, South Carolina went through something called the dispensary system.

In Charleston, temperance is a four-letter word. Many other counties in the state went "dry" during the antebellum years, but despite the presence of numerous temperance organizations, Charleston remained wringing, sopping wet. Ben Tillman wanted to change that. Tillman had two archenemies: the editor of *The State* newspaper, N.G. Gonzales (later murdered by Tillman's cousin) and Charleston. He loathed the

Charleston bourbon dynasty, which had controlled the state's political landscape for two hundred years.

Benjamin R. Tillman, an Edgefield County farmer, was elected South Carolina governor in 1890. In 1894, he was elected Democratic U.S. senator from South Carolina. It was while he was a senator that he earned the nickname "Pitchfork" Ben after he threatened to stick a pitchfork into President Cleveland.

Tillman grew up the youngest of eleven children in a family that had a colorful history, to say the least. His father once killed a man during an argument. His brother John was killed in a duel. Brother Oliver was killed in a "domestic dispute." Brother George, an Edgefield lawyer who was elected to state legislature and U.S. Congress, survived several duels but was later killed in a gambling dispute. Brother Thomas was killed in the Mexican War.

Tillman learned politics during Reconstruction. He hated two things: Republicans and Negroes who were not subservient. He was involved in the execution of a black state senator, Simon Coker. Two of Tillman's men executed Coker with a shot to the head. Tillman ordered that a second shot was needed just in case he was "playing possum." Tillman believed that seven blacks should be killed in retaliation of the death of one white man.

Tillman believed that a reformed Republican was no better than a corrupt Republican. They were both guilty of trying to endow blacks, something Tillman could not accept. He worked hard to rid South Carolina of the Republican/Yankee rule. Tillman admitted that he was committed to "a settled purpose to provoke a riot and teach the Negroes a lesson [by] having the whites demonstrate their superiority by killing as many of them as was justifiable."

Tillman began to attract statewide attention through his diatribes against blacks, bankers and aristocrats, who he claimed were running and ruining the state. Tillman believed that farmers were "butchering the land by renting to ignorant lazy Negroes."

During the 1890 campaign for governor, Tillman was invited to speak in Charleston. The elite white Charleston political machine called Tillman the "hillbilly upstart". Tillman hated Charleston, but he knew the city controlled the most powerful political machine in the state. Many who lived in the upcountry were more conservative and religious and looked down on Charleston. Ben Robertson wrote in *Red Hills and Cotton* that Charleston had been "hard on us for a hundred and ten years."

Charleston was "a worldly place...sumptuous, with the wicked walking on every side."

Tillman addressed a crowd of several thousand from the steps of Charleston City Hall and called the crowd cowards for submitting to the tyranny of elite rule. He began thus:

> *You Charleston people are a peculiar people. If one-tenth of the reports that come to me are true, you are the most arrogant set of cowards that ever drew the free air of heaven. You submit to a tyranny that is degrading you as white men...If anybody was to attempt that thing in Edgefield, I swear before Almighty God we'd lynch him...You are the most self-idolatrous people in the world. I want to tell you that the sun doesn't rise and set in Charleston.*

Over the next hour he called Charleston "the greedy old city." He derided the citizens as "broken-down aristocrats" who viewed the world through "antebellum spectacles" and who "marched backwards when they marched at all." He denounced "that niggerdom" of the Lowcountry.

The hostility Charleston felt toward Governor Tillman turned to outright hatred when Tillman announced the formation of the State Dispensary Board. There had been a liquor prohibition referendum on the 1890 ballot. Of the thirty-five counties in South Carolina, twenty-six of them voted for statewide prohibition. Charleston, of course, was one of the eight counties opposing the referendum. The upstate of South Carolina was more conservative and fundamental than the Lowcountry, and they frowned on drinking and gambling. A tempestuous legislative session over prohibition began in September and at 5:30 a.m. on December 24, 1890, the South Carolina Dispensary Act was passed.

The dispensary was a statewide, state-owned liquor monopoly and was intended to close down all saloons and liquor wholesalers forever, and to restrict the sale of alcoholic beverages to state-operated dispensaries. The board (the governor, comptroller general and attorney general) appointed county dispensary boards, which chose one dispenser per county seat. Due to their larger populations, the cities of Charleston and Columbia could have more, ten and six dispensers respectively. No children or habitual drunkards were allowed to make a purchase. All buyers must register before purchasing liquor. Alcohol could be sold only between the hours of sunrise to sunset. No private citizen could legally manufacture or sell whiskey. Druggists could buy liquor or alcohol from the local dispenser for medicinal purposes.

The people of Charleston were outraged by the law, not only because they considered it to be "Tillman's baby," but because of their 250 year opposition to any regulation of their liquor. Tillman commented about his dispensary system during a speech in Charleston:

> *Why do Charlestonians hate me anyhow? Because they are behind the times and because their streetcars are run by mules instead of electricity. They can go to the devil in their own way if they want to. I am going to have the Dispensary down here whether you want it or not...I will make the places that won't accept the Dispensary dry enough to burn.*

On July 1, 1893, the State Dispensary Board opened for business. Two weeks later, Vincent Chicco, a Charleston Italian saloonkeeper, was arrested on a charge of selling beer to J.H. Pepper, a detective. A group of officers, led by Pepper, arrived with a search warrant to arrest Chicco and search his shop. Chicco began to curse, calling Pepper a "sneaky son-of-a-bitch." A crowd gathered on the street and they joined Chicco in hurling epithets at the officers. Even small children joined in. Chicco was arrested and posted a $500 bond.

The quantity of liquor supplied by the dispensary was not enough to keep Charleston "wet." Nature abhors a vacuum, so a bootleg whiskey industry was soon thriving. Chicco became one South Carolina's most notorious liquor dealers, importing fine liquor from other states. He served on Charleston City Council for four terms and once even sat on a grand jury investigating liquor violations. In other words, Chicco sat on a grand jury that was investigating himself! Chicco was so connected with illegal whiskey that when Governor Tillman criticized drunken behavior in Charleston he called it "raising hell on Chicco Street." Tillman claimed, "There is hardly a train entering the state, day and night, passenger or freight, which does not have contraband liquor." Tillman claimed that half the liquor being consumed in Charleston never passed through the state dispensary.

Tillman authorized state constables to enforce the law, often with little supervision. The constables were heavy-handed in their enforcement, searching private homes on the slightest context and spying on their neighbors. In dozens of cases, the constables killed several citizens but were promptly pardoned by Governor Tillman.

After Chicco was elected as a city alderman he accumulated political power, particularly among the local police. When he was once again raided by the state police he "cursed them so violently, one of the state police drew his gun." Chicco ordered local cops to arrest the state policeman for disturbing the peace. The local constable arrested the state policeman, who was handcuffed and transported to the city jail.

In response to those tactics, Charlestonians began to attack constables by ambush, lying in wait for them armed with clubs and whips. Tillman told the state legislature, "Almost all the people of Charleston are in league against the law and determined to overthrow it." He stated, "The law is going to be enforced. If it results in killing somebody, it will have to be done, that is all."

Law-abiding citizens took pride in resisting the tyranny of the dispensary. They had always enjoyed rum, beer, wine and whiskey in public bars and restaurants; they simply ignored the dispensary law. Illegal bars, called "Blind Tigers," sprung up around the city and prominent citizens engaged in illicit liquor traffic.

Another prominent bootlegger was W.J. Cantwell, brother of the Charleston chief of police. Most of the city leaders opposed the dispensary and looked the other way at violations, or often facilitated the flagrant flaunting of the law.

In April 1894, the South Carolina Supreme Court (by a vote of two to one) ruled the dispensary an illegal monopoly. In Charleston, a triumphant parade marched through the streets. Hundreds of men marched behind a wagon containing a whiskey barrel adorned with a garland of flowers.

When the dispensers closed on April 21, 1894, a flood of liquor poured into South Carolina and Charleston. During the next five months, twelve hundred liquor licenses were issued to private citizens. All the old dealers who had not left the state began to stockpile supplies. People that had never been in the whiskey business began to sell liquor in barbershops, hardware stores, and crossroad grocery stores. However, Governor Tillman was prepared. A new bill passed the state assembly and when the two judges who voted against the dispensary came up for renewal, Tillman replaced them with two of his friends and the new law was declared constitutional on October 8, 1894. The dispensary was too successful (monetarily) to cease. During its thirteen-year existence, its profits exceeded $10 million.

The dispensary quickly came under attack due to corruption among dispensary officials. The board was subject to bribes from various dealers to buy particular brands of liquor. The distillers were ready to give handsome "gifts." Local officials were bribed to overlook the Blind Tigers.

In 1896, in an attempt to clean up the corruption, the dispensary board changed its directors from the governor and other state officials to men elected by the legislature. Soon there were hundreds of people in the state capital schmoozing legislators to become members of the dispensary board, bribing for the right to get their hands on the "liquor money."

Also in 1896, due to flagrant and successive dispensary violations, Tillman's successor, Governor John Evans, placed Charleston under state police control. Evans appointed his own police commissioners and for over a year the city of Charleston's law enforcement was under state control. The result was an improvement in the enforcement of liquor laws, but a growing dissatisfaction among most of the locals who were affected by that enforcement. Twenty-three Protestant ministers issued a statement endorsing the improvement in law enforcement, but the letter was not published by the *News and Courier*, which opposed the state constable rule. For some, the dispensary was seen as a complete and massive failure. Its intention had been to institute a quasi-prohibition, but it had only succeeded in increasing alcohol consumption. In 1898, the prohibitionists (the Drys) made a strong run for the governorship but failed.

In 1905, the South Carolina General Assembly finally decided to investigate the corruption of the dispensary system. Some of the violations included distillers putting more bottles in cases and ordering them as a "gift" to dispensary employees, dispensary inspectors signing blank invoices for a fee, members of the dispensary board being paid an average of $30,000 from the liquor dealers, dispensary workers drinking on the job and dispensary employees selling quarts at an inflated rate and pocketing the seventy-five-cent difference.

The dispensary was repealed by the legislature and thereafter, each county was free to continue its own dispensary system or adopt total prohibition. Under the new system, each county could have as many dispensary licenses as they wanted. In 1906, the state of South Carolina granted 297 liquor licenses; 213 of them were issued in Charleston. Fifteen bars were located around city hall and nineteen operated within a block of St. Philip's Church.

The Reverend Arthur Crain wrote in 1900:

> *The city is wide open. No liquor law is being enforced. Drunkenness greets us on every hand. I can meet more drunken men in a 15-minute walk in Charleston than I could in New York, Chicago or any other city. Speak to the local police who are paid to protect you. They will*

tell you they have no orders to interfere. Why? Because there is no jury around here that will convict them.

The worldwide Spanish influenza epidemic struck Charleston in September 1918. A city official wrote, "whole families were stricken, with no one to look after them; they suffered from lack of food, medicine and clothing." Schools, churches and theatres were shut down and all public social gatherings were banned. The prime antidote, whiskey, was legalized and prescribed to fight the disease. Of the 18,500 infected, less than 500 died.

Governor Coleman Blease (1910–14) had the backing of the whiskey and gambling interests. Blease was popular in Charleston due to his slack attitude towards prostitution, drinking and gambling. He openly endorsed lynching as "necessary and good." Blacks were the primary object of lynching but the governor also stated he would pardon any father who killed a physician for giving his daughter a physical exam without parental consent. He strongly resisted the 1912 law that prohibited horse racing. Charleston, of course, ignored the horse-racing ban. In fact, the manager of the Charleston racetrack was quoted in the Cincinnati *Enquirer* as saying that racing would continue since Charleston had a long history of ignoring laws it did not like. During his second inauguration Governor Blease defended his actions: "They are yelling, 'What is the Governor going to do about the Charleston races?' Do they expect me to dress up like a preacher and beg them not to race?" He continued to ignore Charleston's violations of racing and drinking. Blease said that "if a man wanted to sin, that was his own business, not the state's."

Blease was another in the long line of corrupt South Carolina governors who flaunted their power. During his term Blease freed more than fifteen hundred convicts, many of whom were guilty of murder (of blacks) and arson (against blacks). He also believed in white supremacy. He denounced several members of the state legislature as being born in *North* Carolina and having Yankee parentage. He opposed education for blacks at white taxpayer's expense. He stated, "I have no fear of Negro contacts, neither for me nor any of my family—for each of them, I am proud to say, is physically able to pull a trigger whenever it should become necessary."

He called newspaper reporters "a dirty set of liars" and praised Lieutenant Governor Jim Tillman's (Ben's cousin) murder of N.G.

RAISING HELL ON CHICCO STREET

Gonzales, editor of *The State* newspaper. Gonzales had been a longtime opponent of Tillman and Blease and their policies. In his newspaper, Gonzales had exposed Jim Tillman as a "proven liar, defaulter, gambler and drunkard." On January 15, 1903, Tillman walked from the Senate chamber and shot the unarmed Gonzales on the street. Tillman was acquitted of murder by claiming self-defense.

Mayor John P. Grace once stated that "It is the role of government to prevent crime, not sin." Most of his constituents agreed with him. In 1913 Charleston had 250 Blind Tigers for a population of about 60,000. Mayor Grace bragged that he had instituted a system where the city fined each liquor operator and bordello fifty dollars every three months. He claimed that it was a fair system. "If I wanted, I could fine them every time they sell a drink," he said. He made no effort to close them down. The fines provided thousands of dollars. In fact, without the liquor and prostitution fines, the city budget would have been in the red. The mayor rarely ordered raids on Blind Tigers, and then it was "just for show." He claimed that "Blind Tigers are too much of the web of life to close them down."

In 1915, the Drys won a statewide referendum ending all legal sale of alcohol within the state, four years before national Prohibition took effect. However, the referendum did not repeal the "Gallon-a-Month" law, which permitted the importation into the state of one gallon per person per month. Men like Vincent Chicco, W.J. Cantrell, Leon Dunlap and Frank "Rumpty Rattles" Hogan were more than happy to fill the void of legal liquor with their bootleg product. By the time national Prohibition was in effect, Chicco and other bootleggers had their distilling and distribution systems organized and operating as smoothly as a Ford assembly line. During Prohibition, more than twenty thousand South Carolinians made a living as bootleggers, moonshiners or rumrunners.

The 1923 mayoral election between Grace and Stoney was a wild affair. Stoney, a successful lawyer, had the support of the Broad Street political ring. He appealed to women voters by asking two women to run on his slate. He was a good speaker, entertaining with a good sense of humor.

Mayor Grace linked Stoney with the KKK. Stoney called Grace a corrupt political boss who was hated elsewhere in the state. Two days before the election, Governor McLeod ordered the National Guard to assist the police in keeping order at the polls. This killed any chance of a Grace victory, since Grace's political machine was masterful at poll manipulation. Grace called the use of soldiers "military despotism."

William Watts Ball wrote that "Outsiders gaze upon a Charleston election with wonderment, sometimes with merriment." An election in Charleston was "a scene of reveling, and immorality, a debasing struggle of bribery, corruption and intrigue."

The final count was Stoney: 6,725, Grace: 5,992.

Stoney became the youngest mayor in Charleston history (at age thirty-four) and he and his law partners wielded large influence; they promised any bootlegger willing to pay their fees immunity from prosecution.

On April 7, 1933, Congress repealed national Prohibition and on the following day Charleston merchants were offering 3.2 percent beer for sale, which violated state law, but no one complained. Mayor Maybank, once called a "drunken sot," announced that it did not "matter whether or not the state legalized the sale of alcohol, since tourists wanted it, and Charleston wanted tourists and we will give liquor to them legal or not." Maybank was later elected governor of South Carolina.

South Carolina legalized the sale of beer and wine, but kept in place the prohibition of distilled alcohol. Restaurants and bars could be licensed to serve wine and beer during the week, until midnight on Saturday and never on Sunday. Since distilled liquor was against state law, there were no legal hours to serve whiskey; hence there was no license to lose by selling it. Distilled liquor was available in Charleston around the clock, seven days a week, much to the dismay of the State Law Enforcement Division (SLED).

From ancient times humans have believed that alcoholic beverages had medicinal value. Those beliefs spread widely after the development of distillation techniques. Physicians prescribed alcohol for all sorts of ailments, from snakebite to disease control. By the early nineteenth century, especially in England, there was widespread use of alcohol in medical treatments of various kinds.

The rise of scientific medicine in the latter part of the nineteenth century led to changing views. By the turn of the century the therapeutic value of alcohol was widely disputed and discredited among practitioners. In 1916, the Pharmacopoeia of the United States of America removed whiskey and brandy from the list of scientifically approved medicines. In 1917 the American Medical Association voted, in a contentious meeting, to support prohibition. The resolution passed at the annual meeting of the American Medical Association in June of 1917 read as follows:

Whereas, We believe that the use of alcohol is detrimental to the human economy and, Whereas, its use in therapeutics as a tonic or stimulant or for food has no scientific value; therefore, Be it Resolved, That the American Medical Association is opposed to the use of alcohol as a beverage; and Be it Further Resolved, That the use of alcohol as a therapeutic agent should be further discouraged.

Nevertheless, the Prohibition laws allowed medicinal use of alcoholic beverages through prescription. Physicians could prescribe distilled spirits, usually whiskey or brandy, on government prescription forms. The government even allowed the limited production of whiskey and its distribution when stocks were low. The law also allowed the distribution of wine for sacramental purposes.

Of course, in Charleston, the pharmacy loophole was manipulated to the fullest effect. Many local pharmacists dispensed liquor in addition to their legitimate medications. Customers would call the pharmacist and ask for their "weekend medicine." "Weekend medicine" cost two dollars a bottle and was delivered by the pint by a teenage boy on a bicycle.

Many Charleston locals could buy their bottles after dark. There were several houses in each neighborhood that sold half-pint bottles through the mail slot in the door. The customer would slip two dollars through the slot, and a half-pint bottle was passed out. That way, both parties could claim ignorance about who was buying and who was selling.

In his book *The Charleston Gospel*, J. Francis Brenner describes the system the city developed for keeping the liquor flowing. Whenever SLED officials came to town to investigate the serving of distilled liquor, they would pay a courtesy call to the Charleston police station, informing the local officers that state constables were in town. Chief of Police Herman Berkman would direct the SLED officers to a couple of small-time "half-pint" dealers working out of their cars. Meanwhile, phone calls would be made from the police department. Two bars would be notified that SLED was in town. In turn, those two bars would call two more bars. Those four bars would contact sixteen bars and within half an hour, the city would be as dry as a Puritan in the Sahara. The whiskey disappeared and when SLED walked through the door, only beer and wine could be found on the premises.

Whenever the city needed alcohol for a social function, officials would instruct Chief Berkman to knock off a few half-pint dealers or request "donations" from some of the better restaurants and clubs. It was also well known that local law enforcement officers would "convoy" moonshiners' cars down Highway 42 from Hellhole Swamp in Berkeley County. For allowing the safe passage of liquor into the Holy City, the officers were paid in pint bottles and cold hard cash, some of which worked its way up the chain of command.

It was a smooth and profitable operation for many years until 1951. That was when patrolman James Chassereau became an informant for the United State government. Federal agents hid in the trunk of Chassereau's police cruiser and recorded conversations between police and bootleggers. Nine policemen, including former Chief of Police Julian Williams, and one city councilman, were arrested and sent to federal prison for violating federal liquor laws.

During the trial, the prosecutor asked Chassereau if, while serving on the county police, he did anything other than "fool with liquor." Chassereau answered, "We made a few traffic cases, and answered burglary calls, but our main business was to catch whiskey cars and get what we could out of them."

Former Chief of Police Williams was defended by Ernest "Fritz" Hollings. Hollings was soon to be elected governor of South Carolina. In 2004, Hollings retired after thirty plus years as a U.S. senator. In his defense of Williams, Hollings stated that "the government conspired with perjurers and blackmailers to present a gory picture of this community and of the defendants."

Williams pleaded "not guilty" to all charges. One of the charges was that he was the owner of a property that dispensed illegal whiskey from a freezer in the back of the building and from the Kelly's Newsstand next door. Kelly's was so well known as a place to buy after-hours liquor that you could call a taxi company and ask them to pick up whiskey and deliver it to your house.

Williams claimed to know nothing about the liquor being handed out on his property. The Reverend John J. McCarthy of Blessed Sacrament Roman Catholic Church testified as a character witness for Williams. Father McCarthy stated, "I know that Julian would not commit a sin of perjury." The Father was not questioned about the *other* sins Julian was inclined to commit.

Williams was convicted and sent to federal prison while the bootleggers continued their profitable business.

Charleston has always been a city that loved its alcohol. From the earliest settlers who arrived with twelve tons of beer, to the Reverend Gideon Johnston who missed his ship because he was drunk on Madeira wine, to the little old blueblood ladies sipping liquor on their piazzas in fine China teacups, Charleston has always been a drinking town with a historical problem.

SELF—DEFENSE CHARLESTON STYLE
RUMPTY RATTLES

As a child Frank Hogan picked up the nickname "Rumpty Rattles." Perhaps Frank had been such an adorable baby that his mother gave him the cutesy moniker. But as he grew into a teenager, the nickname "Rumpty Rattles" did not apply to the roughneck man he had become.

Rumpty grew up in a neighborhood of Charleston once called Little Mexico, just outside the city dump. The people in Little Mexico were blue-collar: dock workers, mechanics and railroad workers. Many of the women made extra money at night entertaining men in their beds. Some of the men also made extra money through some extracurricular activities like bootlegging and operating several Blind Tigers.

By the time he was a teenager, Rumpty was doing bootleg running for those men (and spending his money with the women upstairs) and by his early twenties he was a foreman of a crew of stevedores on the Charleston docks. Rattles was a rugged man with a quick temper and anvil fists, which helped to control the rough white and black men in his crew. He had a reputation for violence. He was arrested several times for beatings and shootings and, once, for shooting a woman who he said "was in my way." He also shot another woman who cursed at him. He had also shot several of his liquor competitors, but he was never charged with a crime. He became known as the best pistol shot in the city. By the time he was thirty, Rumpty was called the governor of Little Mexico. He was also often referred to as "that son of a bitch Rattles."

Rumpty liked to carry two guns. During arguments he would toss one pistol on the ground and challenge the man to grab the gun before Rattles could pull his out of his pocket. He would tell his opponent, "Go ahead, pick it up, I've got another." If the man refused Rumpty would tell them, "If you don't go for it, I'll beat the hell out of you." Rattles was not a man to cross. It was a well-known fact that once Rattles said he was going to get you, he probably would.

At night he was a bare-knuckle boxer on the club circuit. Although he often won, Rattles considered beating the hell out of people more of a hobby than a means to make money. He was doing quite well through his contacts on the docks, skimming goods and money where he could, and distributing moonshine to the Blind Tigers throughout the Charleston area. At some point, Rattles opened several of his own Blind Tigers with colorful names like the Robbers Inn, the Bucket of Blood and the Knock Down and Drag Out, which was called "a notorious den for Negroes."

Rattles married and had a young daughter with his wife, but he always kept at least one girlfriend on the side. Rattles liked his girlfriends between the age of eighteen and twenty. When they reached twenty, Rumpty dumped them and found another teenage girl. Even though he was not a handsome man, he kept himself in shape, bleached his hair blond and always had money to spend on his girls. Well into his fifties, Rattles had no trouble finding girls.

He finally got tired of paying protection money to the local cops, so Rattles became "involved" in politics, which meant he bribed voters to vote for the correct candidates and was given a position on the Charleston police force. It was more of an honorary position since no one expected Rattles to show up for a shift. He was given a uniform, a badge and gun, and the unspoken order to do the bidding of the mayor. Once Rattles had a job in the police department and was part of the fraternity, he no longer had to pay bribes and protection money.

Even though he had a reputation as a ruthless criminal, Rattles ran his home at 16 Blake Street as a free flophouse and soup kitchen. Bums and transients slept in his yard and Rattles's wife kept a fifty-gallon lard can of soup simmering on a fire on the back porch, free for anyone who wanted a meal.

Rumpty Rattles's name was entered in the Congressional Record in October 1913. He was not a member of Congress. He never held elective office, even though he was heavily "involved" in politics. The U.S. Congress was investigating the election of Richard S. Whaley to the First District of South Carolina: Rumpty's district. It had been a nasty election. Whaley's brother-in-law was former Mayor Goodwyn Rhett, a longtime political foe of Mayor Grace. Grace was backing Edward Hughes against Whaley. There were charges on both sides of vote buying and intimidation, so the congressional committee got involved.

Rattles testified before Congress that he was a policeman (he had been on the force eleven days), and he was also in the "restaurant and saloon business." Rattles was accused of vote buying. Whaley's supporters testified that in Rumpty's polling district, the first question he asked each voter was, "How much do you want" to vote for Hughes?

RAISING HELL ON CHICCO STREET

Rattles returned home from Washington to operate his liquor business, going into a partnership with Leon Dunlap but the two men separated on bad terms several years later. Rattles then hired a young man to work for him, David Riggs. Riggs was not from Charleston, but from a nearby small town. Rumpty called him "Country Boy." But the Country Boy quickly picked up the ways of the city, and soon he was one of Rumpty's most successful salesmen. He also married Rumpty's eighteen-year-old daughter Marie, proving that *this* Country Boy was no fool. The best way to advance in the company was to marry the boss's daughter. Soon the Country Boy son-in-law was handling most of Rumpty's wholesaling business.

Rumpty's former partner, Dunlap, was also doing well. Dunlap was the exact opposite of Rattles: a small man, fifteen years younger and not at all athletic. Dunlap worked hard to be successful. He imported whiskey not just from the White brothers in Hell Hole Swamp, but also from suppliers from as far away as Savannah. By 1927, corn whiskey was selling at about four dollars per gallon. Dunlap was in the wholesaling liquor business, while Rattles was both retailing and wholesaling.

In October 1927, the White brothers, Lottie and Fulton, made a trip from Hell Hole Swamp into Charleston. The Whites were in town to inform all their bootleg wholesalers that they were raising the price of their whiskey fifty cents a gallon. The Whites first called on Dunlap and Riggs, who were both middlemen for whiskey distribution. The Whites proposed that all four men notify all their retailers in town together. Dunlap did not want to be the one to tell Rattles about the price increase. "We don't get along too good," Dunlap told the White brothers.

The Whites drove to Rumpty's house with Dunlap and Riggs in the back seat. Lottie White informed Rattles of the price increase on their whiskey. Rumpty became enraged, especially when he saw his former partner, Dunlap, in the back seat of the car sitting next to his son-in-law. Rattles called Dunlap a "big-bellied son of a bitch," and Riggs a "long-legged country son of a bitch...trying to take bread out of my mouth. If you get out the car I'll beat the hell out of both of you!"

Riggs and Dunlap both knew that Rattles carried a gun in his pocket. They both slunk down in the backseat, trying not to provoke Rumpty any more until the Whites drove off, with Rattles standing in the yard cursing and threatening them. All the neighbors heard the threats. "I'll get you," he screamed. "Both of you!"

Less than an hour later, Dunlap and Riggs drove Dunlap's Cadillac to

Lindstedt's sporting goods store. "I'm tired of that son of a bitch," Dunlap told Riggs. He then went inside the store and purchased a shotgun for fifty-five dollars along with several buckshot shells. He loaded the gun and for the remainder of the afternoon he and Riggs drove around the city with Riggs behind the wheel and Dunlap literally riding shotgun.

Sometime after nine p.m., Dunlap and Riggs arrived on Market Street, which was a late night hangout for sailors, gamblers, flappers, prostitutes and college boys. There were several restaurants and Blind Tigers in the Market, one of which was a Chinese establishment called the Peking Chop Suey. The Peking sat two doors east of King on the northern side of Market Street (approximately the current location of the Godiva Chocolate shop in the Charleston Place complex). Rumpty's latest girlfriend, eighteen-year-old Myrtle Carter, was employed at the Peking as a waitress, and Rattles usually picked her up after work at one a.m.

Across the street from the Peking was a vacant store (141 Market Street) with a doorway on the street that opened onto a flight of stairs. On the second floor there was a toilet that was used by a restaurant next door. A streetlight shone right over the entrance of the Peking, but the storefront across the street was in the shadows.

Dunlap and Riggs entered the empty building, climbed the stairs and settled down to wait in the bathroom, peering through the small open window. Several people saw them during their forty-five-minute wait for Rattles to appear to pick up Myrtle. Since Dunlap and Riggs were liquor salesmen, many people knew them by sight.

Riggs had to leave around ten o'clock to meet the ferry on the Cooper River, bringing in a load of whiskey from Hell Hole Swamp, but by midnight, he assumed his place next to Dunlap…waiting for Rumpty.

About 1:00 a.m. on October 25, 1927, Rattles parked his car on Market Street and walked to the well-lighted front door of the Peking Chop Suey. Someone shouted, "Rattles, got your gun?" Rumpty turned toward the sound, with his hand in the air, and then there was the explosion of a gunshot. Rattles collapsed in the doorway of the Peking.

Several police who were patrolling the area by foot came running down the street. Dunlap walked out of the empty storefront with the shotgun in his hands. The police grabbed him. Dunlap handed the gun to the cops and told them, "I shot him. The son of a bitch was trying to get me all the God damn day. He's been giving me hell and I'm glad I got him." A moment later Dunlap told Policeman Thompson, "If you had been in the same place, you'd have done the same thing."

Riggs was also grabbed by the cops, but he denied any part of the shooting. Being the son-in-law, the police tended to believe Riggs when he claimed he had nothing to do with it. "Wrong place, wrong time," Riggs said.

The murder of Rumpty Rattles was played up by the local newspapers. It was also picked up by the wire services and splashed around the country. Dunlap and Riggs were arraigned on November 22. Riggs pleaded "not guilty" and Dunlap refused to enter a plea, so the clerk entered the plea of "not guilty" for him. The trial opened on December 19.

During the first morning the jury pool was announced by the court clerk pulling names out of a box. Defense lawyer Russell McGowan had stationed five men in the courthouse. As each name was announced one of the five men would run down Broad Street to McGowan's law office, carrying the name and address of the prospective juror. In the office, ten more men were waiting. These men had the job of locating the juror at his home or work. McGowan's men would engage the potential juror in conversation and without disclosing the fact that the man might be called, they quickly brought up the popular subject of Rumpty's murder and would soon learn how each prospective juror stood on the issue of Rumpty's murder and Dunlap's role in the killing. Nearly two hundred names were pulled for the jury pool.

Judge J.K. Henry wanted the trial to be over before Christmas so he imposed a long session. Court was to run from 9:30 a.m. until 10:00 p.m. with a recess for lunch and dinner. It took two days to seat a jury and then the prosecution presented its case. Twenty-six witnesses were called by the solicitor in one day. The jury heard the story of the shooting of Rattles, the cursing he gave Dunlap and Riggs, the bill of sale for the shotgun and shells and other aspects of the case. The state rested its case at 10:30 p.m. on December 21.

The next morning Mr. McGowan began the defense. McGowan's plan was to put the character of Rattles on trial in order to make the jury come to the conclusion that Rattles was such a bad man that it was no real crime that he was killed.

The jurors were surprised to discover that the two women sitting next to Riggs were Rumpty's widow and daughter, Riggs' mother-in-law and wife. Both women testified that Rattles was a bad man, mean and prone to violence. The widow testified that her husband had died "in his sins" and she was not surprised. The jury heard Myrtle Carter testify that she was separated from her husband and was the mother of a child, but she was the girlfriend of Rumpty Rattles and that he picked her up every night.

In his closing remarks McGowan stressed that the deceased's closest relatives had testified for the defense, not for the prosecution. He stressed that it was only two days from Christmas, and surely the jury did not want to be sequestered away from their families during the holiday, so the only way to avoid that was to bring a quick judgment of "not guilty."

The solicitor told the jury "If you can believe that a man hiding on the second floor of a building in the shadows, firing at a man's back across the street constitutes self-defense, then by all means, render a verdict of 'not guilty.' However if, as reasonable thinking men, you find that to be outrageous and unbelievable, you must return a verdict of 'guilty.'"

The jury retired at 1:02 p.m., December 23. Exactly eleven hours later, at 12:02 a.m., Christmas Eve morning, the jurors returned the outrageous and unbelievable verdict of "Not guilty."

"I am very grateful," Dunlap told the newspapers.

"Boy, I'm the happiest man in the world," declared Riggs.

"Happy, that's all," said his wife.

Not for long. They later divorced and Riggs married another woman. That marriage soon broke up and Riggs left Charleston and returned to the country.

Dunlap went back to the bootleg liquor industry. He was later imprisoned for violating the federal ban on Prohibition, and in 1936, he was indicted in federal court for ten violations of income tax evasion. He served five years in a federal penitentiary. During the tax trial, newspapers referred to Dunlap as "the biggest moonshine liquor operator in Charleston" and the acquitted murderer of Frank "Rumpty Rattles" Hogan.

McGowan, the lawyer, built his reputation on the trial. After all, he was able to convince a jury to acquit a confessed killer. He later ran for the solicitor's job and was elected. The only payment he claimed he ever got for defending Dunlap was the shotgun used to shoot that son-of-a-bitch Rattles. The McGowan family still owns the gun.

In 1927, self-defense in Charleston meant you could shoot a man in the back, across a dark street from a second floor window as long as he was a son of a bitch.

Author's Note: The Twenty-first Amendment, which was ratified in 1933, repealed the Eighteenth Amendment. In order to get around the traditional process of ratification by the state legislatures—many of which were expected

to vote "dry"—Congress instead called for ratifying conventions in each state.
At the completion of delegates' voting, the national count in favor of repeal of
the Eighteenth Amendment was 73 percent.

THAT'S WHERE THE MONEY IS

At approximately 7:00 p.m. on January 17, 1950, seven armed men walked into the Prince Street entrance of the Brinks Building in Boston. Each man was carrying a pistol, wearing a navy-type pea coat, chauffeur's cap and wearing a Halloween-type mask. Each carried a pair of gloves. One man, Joseph "Specs" O'Keefe wore crepe-soled shoes to muffle his footsteps; the other men wore rubber boots.

The men quickly entered the Brinks building and donned their masks. Within half an hour the seven men had looted the premises of $1.2 million in cash and $1.5 million in checks, money orders and other securities. By prior agreement the seven men handed their stolen money over to a mafia syndicate for safekeeping. Their agreement was not to touch the money for at least seven years, when the statute of limitations for the crime would have passed. The seven men then scattered.

It was the largest bank robbery in the United States at the time and came to be known as the Great Brinks Robbery. It took the FBI six years to crack the case. Two motion pictures and countless books have been written about the robbery and its aftermath. What is not well known, however, is Charleston's connection with the Great Brinks Robbery and some of the mobsters who ended up living down south.

Soon after the robbery, the police were hot on the trail of every known crook and thief in Boston. Some of the early suspects included Joseph "Specs" O'Keefe, Henry Baker, Anthony Pino, Joseph McGinnis and Stanley Gusciroa. Six months after the Brinks job, O'Keefe was arrested in Pennsylvania. The police discovered stolen merchandise in his car, unrelated to the Brinks job. O'Keefe was sentenced to three years in the Bradford, Massachusetts, County Jail for robbery. During O'Keefe's confinement law enforcement officials kept hearing rumors that O'Keefe was putting pressure on the Boston mob to release his take of the Brinks money in order to pay for his legal problems in Bradford County. The FBI began to put pressure on O'Keefe, hoping he could rat out the Brinks gang. O'Keefe steadfastly denied any knowledge of the Brinks robbery. In fact, in December of 1952, almost three years after the Brinks job, a federal grand jury held hearings and issued a report that there was not sufficient evidence to indict anyone for the Brinks robbery. The FBI was more frustrated than ever.

O'Keefe finished his sentence in Bradford County and was taken to McKean County to stand trial for burglary and receiving stolen goods. He was released on $17,000 bond. While free, O'Keefe continued his attempts to get his Brinks money. He was becoming bitter toward some of his partners. On June 5, 1954, O'Keefe was driving in Dorchester, Massachusetts, when another automobile pulled alongside him. Immediately suspicious, O'Keefe crouched down low in the front seat just as several bullets shattered his windshield.

On June 14, O'Keefe paid a visit to Henry Baker, one of the Brinks partners. Baker was getting nervous about O'Keefe's constant visits. Baker pulled a pistol and shots were exchanged between the two men, but no one was injured.

Two days later, O'Keefe was attacked in his neighborhood, a quiet housing complex off Victory Road. A slender man carrying a machine gun sprayed bullets at O'Keefe, who took off in a run. For the next half hour, O'Keefe was chased through the neighborhood, over fences, through backyards and alleys, with the machine blasts peppering buildings and trees. When the police sirens finally began to wail in the distance, the shooter fled. O'Keefe had been shot in the chest and arm, but he was still alive. At the scene the police discovered a lot of blood, a man's shattered wristwatch and a .45-caliber pistol. They also discovered five bullets lodged in a building nearby.

Thomas F. Mulvoy Jr. of *The Boston Globe* staff reminisced about the event.

> *I was eleven years old at the time and living five streets away from Victory Road. I remember well walking down to Victory Road the next day after reading as many newspapers as I could. With scores of other curious onlookers, I tried to come to grips with the awesome shootout that had made our quiet neighborhood temporarily notorious.*

On June 17, 1954, eight days after the shootout, Boston patrolman Frank Crawford arrested Elmer Francis "Trigger" Burke in the exclusive Back Bay section of the city and charged him with possession of a machine gun. This machine gun was quickly identified as having been used in the attempt on O'Keefe's life. Police assumed that Burke, a professional killer, had been hired by underworld associates to assassinate O'Keefe.

After being wounded in the shootout, O'Keefe disappeared for seven weeks. He was arrested on August 1 in Leicester, Massachusetts, and turned over to Boston police for violating parole on a gun-carrying charge. Remarkably, O'Keefe swore out a complaint against Trigger Burke for attempted murder!

ELMER FRANCIS "TRIGGER" BURKE
MACHINE GUN FOR HIRE

Elmer Francis "Trigger" Burke was raised in New York by his brother Charlie, who had taken over care of the family after the death of their parents. Soon the two brothers were committing petty robberies in their neighborhood. Trigger was sent to reform school in 1941, but his sentence was reduced when he joined the army. He served in Italy during World War II, became an army ranger and became proficient in the use of a machine gun. He was awarded the Bronze Star Medal, the Combat Infantryman's Badge, the American Theatre and Europe-Africa-Middle Eastern ribbons with three battle stars. Most ironically, Trigger also won the Good Conduct Medal. After the war he returned to New York and during the late 1940s Trigger became a busy hit man for hire, specializing in machine gun killings. He hated his given name, Elmer Francis, and preferred his nickname, "Trigger."

In 1946 Trigger was arrested after robbing a liquor store. He was arrested by police while sitting in the car outside the store counting the loot. He was sentenced to two years in Sing Sing Prison.

During Trigger's stay in Sing Sing, his brother, Charlie, was killed during a mob gun battle. Trigger swore vengeance for his brother's death, even though no one ever knew who the killer was. No matter to Trigger. Upon his release from Sing Sing, Trigger hunted down the man he suspected of killing Charlie and shot the man point blank in the back of the head with a double-barreled shotgun. With his personal business completed Trigger went back into the killer-for-hire business. His standard fee for a mob hit was $1,000. Trigger became known for his efficiency and utter lack of compassion. He also became known for his volcanic temper.

One night in a New York tavern, Trigger got into an argument with another man. Within a few moments Trigger had beat the man to the floor and was kicking him repeatedly in the head with his boot. The bartender,

Edward "Poochy" Walsh, stepped in and stopped Trigger. Poochy ordered Burke out of the bar.

"If he's not dead yet, he might as well be," Poochy told Trigger. "Now, get outta here!"

Trigger went outside and smoked a cigarette. Ten minutes later he walked back in the tavern, pulled out a pistol and shot Poochy Walsh in the face twice. He then stepped around the bar and shot the already-dead Poochy again in the face. "He shoulda minded his own bidness," Trigger told the stunned crowd, and then he calmly strolled out.

In 1954, the mob hired Trigger to go to Boston and kill Specs O'Keefe before he ratted out the Brinks Robbery gang. After the Victory Road shooting spree Trigger did not leave town. He spent the next few days viewing the historic sites: Bunker Hill, the Old North Church and Paul Revere's house. When he was arrested Trigger was touring the mansions of Back Bay with the machine gun hidden beneath his jacket.

He was held in Suffolk County jail, but on the afternoon of August 28, Trigger escaped. During the regular exercise period, Trigger walked away from the rest of the prisoners and walked toward a heavy steel door that lead to the solitary confinement section. A guard hollered for him to stop, and Trigger began to run. The steel door opened and a masked gunman wearing a prison guard uniform ordered the guard to "Back up, or I'll blow ya brains out!" Trigger and the gunman fled through the door and escaped in a nearby parked automobile.

The automobile was later traced to Anthony Pino, one of the original Brinks gang. Police questioned Pino, but he denied any knowledge of Trigger's escape.

Less than a week later Trigger arrived in Charleston and began to look for rental property on the Isle of Palms. During the search for a rental Trigger was accompanied by Thomas "Duke" Connelly Jr. Connelly had been the getaway driver in the $305,000 robbery of the Woodside branch of the Chase Manhattan bank in Queens, New York. Connelly had made it onto the FBI's Most Wanted List and he had chosen the Isle of Palms as an out-the-way hiding place in which to spend his share of the $90,000 loot.

Driving a car they had borrowed from Isaac "Issy" Sabel, a Charleston nightclub owner with New York mob ties and famous for his Manischevitz Popsicles, the two men introduced themselves as "friends of Mr. Sabel" and told a real estate agent that "money was no object." Connelly rented a house under the alias "Mr. Kelly," using Issy Sabel's name as a reference, and they moved in with Connelly's wife, Ann, and their two small children. Trigger and Duke quickly became familiar faces on the Isle of Palms.

For several months, Trigger and Duke lived a good life, spending their money fishing, swimming and boating. The two men even joined the YMCA Health Club where they mingled with the mayor, policemen and other city officials like Judge Ashton Williams. They also spent many evenings hanging out in Issy Sable's nightclub on Market Street, drinking and being entertained by Issy's girls.

When Trigger mentioned he wanted new clothes, Issy sent them to the best store in Charleston, Berlin's Men's Wear on King Street. Henry Berlin personally outfitted the two mobsters with the best suits, shirts and other attire. When it came time to purchase the shoes Trigger told Mr. Berlin he wore a size nine. Mr. Berlin protested. "A big man like you must have a larger foot." With an icy glare, Trigger told Berlin he wore a size nine. Months later, talking with the FBI, Henry Berlin related the shoe story. The FBI agent told Mr. Berlin he was lucky. Trigger had been known to kill people for less provocation—like bartender Poochy Walsh.

On June 27, 1955, Duke Connelly and his family vanished. A month later the two children were discovered abandoned, one in Wilmington, Delaware, and the other in Baltimore, Maryland. No one ever saw Duke or his wife again. Local rumor persisted that Trigger had discovered where Duke was hiding his $90,000 and decided to make some easy money for himself. There was also a rumor that the money was never recovered and for years afterward, people dug thousands of holes on the island looking for Duke's money.

In July, under the name of "Mr. Dean," Trigger rented a cottage on Folly Beach, at 109 Erie Avenue, diagonally across the street from the Folly Beach police department. Unbeknownst to Trigger, on the next block was the beach house of the Charleston police chief of detectives and the home of the former county police commissioner. Trigger hired a local black woman, Annabelle Richardson, to keep house for him. She claimed Trigger told her he was from New York and was living in Folly Beach as he recovered from an operation. Annabelle described him as an "avid television fan and a frequent reader of local newspapers and 'gentlemen' magazines." Annabelle later told the FBI that she noticed her boss always kept the doors and windows locked, even during the middle of summer.

Trigger became a familiar face on the island, taking afternoon strolls along the beach and boulevard. He made a lot of purchases in town, always paying cash. He bought a twenty-one-inch screen floor model television, a new washing machine, an electric fan and wall clock. Trigger even donated fifty cents to the Junior Deputies League when they knocked on his door collecting money.

On August 27, 1955, Trigger walked into a trap set by the FBI. Local law enforcement had become mildly suspicious of Trigger and finally identified him through an FBI wanted poster. They began a round-the-clock stakeout of his house. He never received mail and the only people who ever visited were the housekeeper, Annabelle, and a "nice-looking blonde of about 26-years old." When he took his usual afternoon stroll he was met at the corner of Erie and Center Streets. A car pulled up and several FBI agents leaped out, armed with machine guns. "We're from the FBI! Are you Elmer Francis Burke?"

Trigger said, "Yes, I am." He offered no resistance when he was taken into custody. When agents searched his house they discovered two .38-caliber pistols and two .22-caliber rifles, one equipped with telescopic sights. Agents described his appearance as casually attired with well-manicured fingernails and "deeply tanned."

He refused extradition to New York so a hearing was scheduled in Charleston, presided over by Judge Ashton H. Williams. Williams said he recognized Trigger the moment he was brought into his courtroom. The judge's Isle of Palms house was three doors down from Duke Connelly's and he had often talked with Trigger and Duke at the YMCA Health Club.

After the hearing Henry Berlin lamented that no one ever mentioned how handsome Trigger looked in his fine suit from Berlin's Men's Wear.

During his trial in New York Trigger was questioned about the whereabouts of Duke Connelly and his wife, Anne. The New York district attorney asked, "Were the Connellys with you at the Folly Beach cottage?"

Trigger responded, "I refuse to answer."

"What happened to the Connellys and their two children?"

"I refuse to answer."

"Who gave you the money to live?"

"I refuse to answer."

Trigger was found guilty of the murder of Edward "Poochy" Walsh and given the death penalty. On January 8, 1958, he was executed at Sing Sing

Prison. Before his execution a reporter asked him why he robbed banks and murdered people, Trigger replied, "That's where the money is."

Specs O'Keefe, the man Trigger was supposed to rub out, was sentenced on August 5, 1954, to serve twenty-seven months in prison on a probation violation. As a protective measure, he was incarcerated in the Hampden County Jail in Springfield, Massachusetts, rather than the Suffolk County Jail in Boston. During his incarceration, with eleven days before the statute of limitations was due to run out for the crime, O'Keefe began to cooperate with the FBI against the rest of the Brinks Robbery gang. Due to his cooperation his sentence was reduced. After his release O'Keefe was given a new identity and moved to Los Angeles. After his death in 1976, it was revealed that O'Keefe had spent his last few years as a chauffeur for Cary Grant.

Author's Note: Ashley Cooper, former columnist for the Charleston News and Courier, was known in real life as Frank Gilbreath Jr., author of the classic memoir Cheaper By the Dozen. Gilbreath, a longtime Charleston resident, weighed in on the Trigger Burke caper in his own inimitable way with this poetic little ditty.

Charleston beaches long have been a haven
For lovers and tourists and the poet who wrote "The Raven."
But the shootingest tourist with the meanest quirk
Was a New York gunman named Trigger Burke.

Trigger had a buddy and shot him dead,
Used a pistol to fill him full of lead
Trigger had another buddy, shady as a spook
Name of Connelly, alias the Duke.

Duke and Trigger preyed upon the yanks,
Took their gold and silver and never gave them thanks.
When the cops put out their big alarms,
Trigger brought Duke to the Isle of Palms.

"Don't fret, buddy," Trigger said to Duke,
"Only time they caught me, it was only a fluke.
Don't fret, buddy," he repeated with a smirk,
"There ain't no jail can hold Mr. Trigger Burke."

Duke must have felt he was in the middle.
What happened to Duke is still a riddle.
But Trigger was afraid the Duke would preach
So Trigger moved over to Folly Beach.

Lived all alone, in a cement house,
Minded his manners, quiet as a mouse.
And all the time he was grinning like a pixie,
"Ain't the cops dumb Down South in Dixie?

"Ain't the cops dumb? And ain' they hicks?
Safest place to be is here in the sticks.
Southern coppers? Well, by golly
They'll never dream that I'm hidin' out at Folly."

But the cops weren't dumb and that's no lie.
'Cause the cops and the sheriff and the FBI
Crept down to Folly, there to lurk,
And trapped like a rat Mr. Trigger Burke.

"Put up your hands," said the FBI.
"Face the wall, Trigger, 'less you want to die.
Burke, you've been acting mighty regal.
Now lie down, Trigger and do the spread eagle!"

Trigger done just like he was told,
Lay down like he was knocked out cold.
But all the time, only one thought lingered,
"I wonder," he grated, "who had me fingered."

"Trigger," said the cops, "it's sad to tell,
We got to take you now to Seabreeze Hotel."
He heard those words and Burke turned pale.
'Cause the Seabreeze Hotel is the county jail.

There's not much more of the story to report
The cops brought Trig to the Charleston Court.

RAISING HELL ON CHICCO STREET

When reporters took his picture, he didn't say "thank ye."
Covered his face with a spotless hankie.

Burke told the judge with a mealy mouth,
"Please, yur honor, can I stay in the South?"
The judge replied with nary a snigger,
"You'll like it up North, Mr. Convict Trigger."

They put Mr. Burke on the train "Champeen,"
And he said with a sneer that was almost obscene.
"What happened to me shouldn't happen to a collie,
When the Southern cops found me hidin' out in Folly."

New Verse (by Mark R. Jones)
Back up North in a prison they call Sing Sing
Trigger discovered a place he could not take wing.
Freedom did happen—not scattered, not smothered, but fried,
In January of 1958, Trigger finally died.

CHAPTER FOUR
STILL DOIN' THE CHARLESTON

THE WAYWARD JUDGE WARING CIVIL RIGHTS HERO

Seven generations of Warings had lived in the Lowcountry before the birth of Waties Waring in Charleston. Waties attended local private schools, graduated from the College of Charleston in 1900 and later passed the bar exam. The early twentieth century cosmopolitan enclave that was Charleston fit Waring like an old comfortable shoe. In college his loftiest goal was to join one of the fraternities that reigned over the social life—a mere reproduction of the adult Charleston community. In his later years, at age seventy-six, Waring commented on the Charleston society of his youth, "Pretty nice if you belong to it, but it's really a terrible social system. It has a charm, a fashion, but it doesn't think much, and it doesn't think outside of its pattern."

He began his law practice in Charleston and quickly developed a reputation as the city's foremost ladies man. In fact, Waring became the most honored patron of the Big Brick. A poem that immortalized Waring was written by his friend, Arthur Jervey Stoney, when Waring was in his twilight years. The framed copy of the poem used to hang on the wall of the bordello:

He was King of the Tenderloin
Big Brick was his palace hall

STILL DOIN' THE CHARLESTON

And the girls were wild with excitement
When the judge was coming to call

The Madam's smile was wide for him
He could charge up any amount
For he was the one patron of the Brick
Who enjoyed a charge account

The judge now old, his youth long spent
Can now only dream and repine
He was master swordsman once
And the Brick shall be his shrine

In 1913, Waring married Annie Gammell, a seventh-generation proper Charleston lady. They belonged to the best clubs; he and Annie were on the list for every prominent social and civic function. Two years later their acceptance in the upper strata of Charleston society became complete when they purchased a restored carriage house at 51 Meeting Street. In the Charleston vernacular, the Warings were now SOBs, with an address south of Broad Street. He became a U.S. attorney and served as the campaign manager for segregationist Senator Ellison "Cotton Ed" Smith. In December 1941, in the culmination of his career, Cotton Ed helped secure Waring's nomination to the federal bench by President Roosevelt.

The judge and Annie were passionate bridge players and they enjoyed frequent card parties at their south of Broad home. Included in their bridge group were the Hoffmans, a well-to-do Detroit couple who spent their winters in their Broad Street mansion. Soon a strong romantic relationship developed between the once-divorced Elizabeth Avery Hoffman and the distinguished Judge Waring. Elizabeth was very much a modern woman, opinionated and intelligent; a sharp contrast to most of the other Charleston-bred women in the Warings' social circle, particularly the very traditional Annie Waring. Elizabeth stated, "They (Charlestonians) love rich Northerners, and I was party material."

Carl Rowan, a nationally syndicated African American columnist, commented on his first encounter with Elizabeth, "She walked down the stairs with elegance that Charleston's *haute monde* could envy, and accorded me a welcome fit for a cavalier."

Elizabeth became good gossip fodder among Charleston women. They liked to complain about her pronouncements on race relations and political issues. Even the Charleston men liked to gossip about Elizabeth. They found her opinions "unbecoming of a lady."

Although the judge had quite a reputation for his ability to romance his secretaries and was the most loved visitor to the local brothels, he became romantically involved with Elizabeth, and in the fall of 1944 he told his wife he wanted a divorce. In a letter written to Annie's sister, Lena Adams Deshilds, the judge explains the divorce:

> *We have ceased all marital relations for which I am solely responsible and to blame...I have convinced her that my mind was definitely made up and, I cannot deny that I have been the cause of breaking up our home since I have told her that I was unwilling that we should any longer share a home...I can only say that we have drifted apart because I have tired of our life together and I wish to get away from it and be free...I have been cruel and brutal to treat her in this manner, but nevertheless, I have determined my course and shall not change.*

The 1895 Constitution had prohibited divorce and by 1947, South Carolina was the only state that did not permit couples to divorce. Attempts to repeal the law had been made in 1916, 1937, 1944 and 1945 with no success. In 1944, to divorce in South Carolina, a couple must separate, and one of the two must establish residency for one year in a state that allowed divorce. However, people who obtained divorces out of state and remarried were legally considered adulterers. Any subsequent children from that marriage were legally bastards and often threw estates into question.

Annie obediently followed the judge's directions. She moved to Florida to establish residency and on June 8, 1945, the divorce was granted in Florida. Annie was given a generous financial settlement, and the judge retained possession of the Meeting Street house. In the meantime, Elizabeth got a quickie divorce from her husband in Nevada. Less than a week after the Warings' divorce was final, the judge married Elizabeth, fifteen years his junior and they moved into the Meeting Street home.

The divorce and subsequent quick marriage rocked Charleston society. Elizabeth was referred to as "some bridge player." An anonymous local attorney told *Collier's* magazine that "something come over him." There were insinuations that the judge was mentally infirm or under demonic possession.

After she became the judge's wife Elizabeth became even *more* outspoken in support of civil rights. Soon the Warings were shunned in Charleston society. Judge Waring was forced to resign from the South Carolina society. When he made the announcement, the room exploded into cheers. Elizabeth attempted to have the old monogram of Annie's silver tea set ground off and a new one engraved, but no silversmith in the city would do the job. When the newly married couple would enter a room at a social function, the room quickly emptied. Elizabeth was snubbed in local shops not only by other women, but also by the clerks. Local waitresses turned their backs on the judge when he sat down for his lunch, and refused to take his order.

In 1948, the *McComb* (Mississippi) *Enterprise-Journal* ran an editorial entitled "Time for a Divorce." It told the tale of a husband cursed with an unfaithful wife; even though the husband had "built a lovely house and showered his wife with affection…she commenced to running around with Tom, Dick and Harry."

> *Then one day Tom, Dick and Harry moved into his house, sat at his table and ordered food from his kitchen and enjoyed every luxury his home afforded. The neighbors looked on with ridicule. They laughed at him. Then one day Tom, Dick and Harry took the husband by the nape of the neck and threw him out into the mud of the street and took over his home, completely. The neighbors looked on in disgust. They had no respect for him.*

This was not a tale of some local couple, but an allegory to the white South's position in the Democratic Party during the post World War II era. Distressed by the landmark civil rights pronouncements by Truman and fearful of being usurped by black voters the Democrats could see they were losing their power within the party. Some Democrats began to play up family values, describing the bastardy and broken marriages that would become rampant due to the prominence of the blacks. These Democrats came to be called the States' Rights Party, or as they were commonly called, the Dixiecrats. Like the husband in the editorial, the Dixiecrats thought they were being usurped within the Democratic Party and wanted to divorce themselves from the party. They worried they were also losing control of their own households because the South Carolina legislature was debating the abolishment of the fifty-two year old ban on marital divorce.

Those against divorce saw it as a further erosion of masculine privilege. One representative said, "Our wives back home are bad enough, and we had better not be giving them any ideas about divorce." The *News and Courier* equated broken families with blacks. The paper stated that if divorce was legal, "divorces in the Negro population will be especially numerous."

A resolution was passed by the assembly allowing for divorce only on the grounds of adultery, desertion, habitual drunkenness or physical cruelty. In 1948, voters approved the referendum and Governor Strom Thurmond signed the bill into law the next year.

Elizabeth began attending her husband's court proceedings. Local lawyers complained that Elizabeth was a distraction for the judge. Joseph Young commented, "When Elizabeth entered the courtroom it was hell. It was no court. Nobody would do anything because he wasn't listening. He wasn't doing anything but paying attention to Elizabeth."

Another confirmation that the judge was mentally infirm occurred in early 1945 when he ruled that segregated seating for jurors was unconstitutional. He also upheld a Supreme Court mandate that public schoolteachers should receive equal pay, regardless of race. Then…the bombshell.

On July 12, 1947, Judge Waties Waring presided over the federal court of the Eastern District of South Carolina in the case of *Elmore v. Rice*. The plaintiff, Elmore, a black man, had not been permitted to vote in the Democratic primary, so he sued for the right. Judge Waring decided for the plaintiff. During the trial the *News and Courier* stated that the Democratic primary functioned like a private organization, "a state-wide collection of white-skinned clubs."

In his decision Waring stated, "Private clubs…do not vote and elect a president. It is time for South Carolina to rejoin the Union. [And] adopt the American way of conducting elections."

Blacks were jubilant, but many whites were angry. Mayor Wehman predicted the end of the Democratic Party "as we have known it." The judge later reminisced that after his decision, a group of his relatives "waited until 2:30 one morning to call and say hello and tell me that they didn't think it wise to see me anymore."

Elizabeth continued her public appearances. She gave a speech to the all-black Coming Street YMCA and described the white Charleston elite as "a sick…and decadent people…so self-centered that they have not considered themselves as part of the country since the Civil War."

On Sunday, February 11, 1950, she appeared on NBC's "Meet The Press" and complained that while other states had made progress in race relations, South Carolina remained "an exact replica of Russia." She also called for intermarriage between whites and blacks.

The following Monday, the South Carolina House of Representatives introduced a resolution to appropriate funds to purchase one-way tickets for the judge and his wife to "any place they desired provided that they never return to the state." The resolution was passed and sent to the state Senate. Judge Waring was in New York at the time and during a speech to a church group he stated, "We don't have a Negro problem in the South; we have a white problem. The white men...are obsessed" with white supremacy. He later stated that "We do not live in the darkest Africa, we live in the darkest South Carolina." Burnet R. Maybank, senator from South Carolina and a Charleston resident, told his friends that Judge Waring was "crazy and should be in an institution."

One month later, a cross was burned in front of the Warings' house. The judge resigned his membership in the St. Cecilia Society and pulled his membership from St. Michael's Church. When Elizabeth would walk around town, she was called "witch" and "prostitute" by local blueblood "ladies." After three shots were fired at the house and a large block of concrete was tossed through the window, Judge Waring was put under round-the-clock protection by federal marshals.

On May 17, 1954, when the U.S. Supreme Court unanimously ruled that "separate but equal" was unconstitutional, Judge Waring's decision was cited as a landmark on the path leading to this decision. White Carolinians were shocked and angered. They were in disbelief.

Judge Waring had a party on the night the "separate but equal" decision was announced. Many claimed that because the judge and his damn Yankee wife had been shunned by Charleston society, he took his vengeance out by ruling against the white elite in civil rights cases. Lena Adams Deshilds, the judge's former sister-in-law, wrote to Waring, "I write to extend to you my profound sympathy in this hour of your humiliation." Letters to the editors raged against the judge.

"Why did you wait until you took on this second wife before you suddenly became mad at all white people?"

"A man who disposes of a woman to whom he had been married for 33 years, against her will, and takes another man's wife...is morally unfit to serve as Judge."

Many doubted Waring's manhood. In the short-sighted eyes of most southern gentlemen and ladies the fact that Waring was unable to control his wife left him emasculated. Letter writers suggested that Waring's civil rights rulings were due to the fact that he was a weak man, his opinions and behavior forced upon him by his Yankee wife. It was a reversal of gender and marital roles that was unacceptable in the South. What opinion the girls at the Big Brick had about the Judge's manhood, once the master swordsman, remains a mystery.

The Warings subsequently moved to New York City. When the judge died in 1968, his body was returned for burial at Magnolia Cemetery. Charles Kuralt of CBS News reported that "there are few white mourners here today." Out of more than two hundred people who attended the burial, less than a dozen were white.

SLEEPING WITH MISS DENMARK, A NAZI SPY

Inga Arvad was born in Copenhagen in June 1913. At the age of fifteen (1928), Inga won the Miss Denmark contest with a thirty-six inch bust, eighteen-inch waist and thirty-five inch hips. While in Paris for the Miss Europe contest, the sixteen-year-old Inga met a young Egyptian student and diplomat with whom she eloped. When his posting in Paris ended and he was recalled to Egypt, she filed for divorce rather than live in dusty, squalid Cairo.

In 1935, during a French Riviera vacation, she won a local beauty contest, which brought her to the notice of Paul Fejos, a Hungarian-born film director who had become an American citizen. Fejos cast Inga in one of his films. After her divorce from the Egyptian diplomat was final in 1936, she married Fejos, who was twice her age, hoping a film career would follow.

It did not. Disillusioned with filmmaking, Inga traveled to Berlin, and using her charm, beauty and sexual wiles she was able to convince the editor of *Berlingske Tidne*, the leading Danish newspaper, to give her credentials as a journalist. With these credentials she was able to meet Emmy Sonneman, Hermann Goering's fiancée; she quickly gained access to the Nazi inner sanctum that any journalist would have envied. She interviewed Joseph Gobbles, Heinrich Hammer, Hermann Goring and Adolf Hitler himself. She later attended Goering's wedding, and in 1936 she attended the Berlin Olympics as a personal guest of Hitler. She even sat in his private box, where a photograph of her was taken sitting with the Fuhrer. Hitler gave Inga a signed photo of himself in a silver and red leather frame with the inscription, "To an indefinite Frau." Hitler rarely gave out personal photos, and it was extraordinary that he gave one to Inga.

While in Berlin, Inga met Axel Wenner-Gren, the richest man in Scandinavia. Wenner-Gren had founded Electrolux and was a prominent interest holder in Bofors, a Swedish arms manufacturer that specialized in guns and light artillery. He also owned five million acres of prime timberland and was an enthusiastic supporter of Hitler. Wenner-Gren took Inga as his mistress.

In 1938, Inga traveled with her husband, Fejos, to the East Indies to film anthropological explorations. There, in the remote villages, Inga claimed she was worshipped as a goddess by the locals and that a primitive statue was built to replicate her blonde statuesque beauty.

Inga soon bored of the primitive lifestyle however, and arrived in New York in February 1940. She enrolled at Columbia University where she took classes in English and journalism. She alienated her Jewish classmates with her outspoken admiration of Hitler and her denunciation of "the goddamned Chews." After spending an evening at Inga's apartment in November 1940, one of her classmates wrote a letter to the FBI

> *The conversation slid into a discussion of the large number of Jews in the class, and the danger of civil war in this country. We left very late, dazed by her charms, but with the uncomfortable feeling that we had somehow been threatened. It seems she has been set up at the school for the purpose of influencing morale in the country for the benefit of the German government.*

The FBI opened a file on Inga and began collecting information.

Even though she was still married to Paul Fejos, Inga was carrying on affairs with several professors as well as with Nils Blok, who worked for the Danish consulate. She had also met and befriended Arthur Krock, the powerful *New York Times* columnist. Upon her graduation from Columbia, Inga moved to Washington, D.C., where Krock recommended her for a job at the *Washington Times-Herald*.

In order to impress her new bosses with her skill as a reporter, Inga arranged an interview with her former lover, Axel Wenner-Gren, multimillionaire and a Nazi sympathizer. Inga was assigned to the paper to write a chatty column profiling the powerful and the intriguing. It was a job at which Inga excelled. Washington was filled with powerful men who fancied pretty women. Inga quickly had dozens of admirers. Powerful men were begging to be interviewed. The job didn't pay much, but Wenner-Gren gave her $5,000 a year allowance. In 1941, the average American annual household income was $2,500.

A young woman named Kathleen, whose father was a former ambassador to England, also worked at the *Washington Times-Herald*. In November of 1941 Kick, as Kathleen was called by her friends, introduced Inga to her brother, Jay. Jay worked at the office of Naval Intelligence, a cushy position procured by the influence of his ambassador father. Jay was instantly attracted to Inga, and she was similarly drawn to him. Jay immediately shifted his attention from another *Times-Herald* reporter, Page Huidekoper, and focused all his energy on Inga. Jay began spending the night at Inga's apartment two or three times a week, and publicly calling her "Inga Binga."

Page, humiliated by Jay's sudden and cold dismissal of her, informed the FBI of Inga's political views and suggested in a letter that Inga may be a Nazi spy. The FBI increased their mild interest in Inga to a full investigation, including twenty-four hour surveillance and wiretaps on her phones. They broke into her apartment and photocopied her letters and other documents.

The information gathered during the FBI investigation immediately began to raise the agents' suspicions about Inga. The agent in charge noted that the case "had more possibilities than anything else I have seen in a long time." Based on their investigation a report was delivered to the desk of FBI director J. Edgar Hoover listing their findings:

1. Inga was personal friends with several high-ranking Nazi officials.

2. She possessed a personally autographed photo of Hitler, and there was another photo of her with Hitler in his Olympic box.

3. She openly defended Hitler in public, spoke of her admiration of the Nazis, and often denounced "the goddamned Chews."

4. She was also the lover of known Nazi sympathizer Wenner-Gren, one of the most successful arms dealers in the world. She had received $5,000 from him this year. Wenner-Gren was also under suspicion for using his yacht (the *Southern Cross*, purchased from Howard Hughes) to help refuel Nazi submarines in the Gulf of Mexico; he also owned a bank in the Bahamas that was known to have laundered money for the Duke of Windsor, another Nazi sympathizer.

5. She had suddenly appeared in New York City two years ago to study journalism, and was now mixing with the elite in Washington, currently having an affair with a young ensign working in the office of Naval Intelligence.

It was Hoover who connected the dots and realized the young ensign cited in the reports as Inga's lover was none other than the former ambassador's son. He immediately sent a report to the chief of naval operations, Admiral Ernie King, that one of his officers in Naval Intelligence was having an affair with a woman suspected of Nazi affiliations.

The day after Hoover reported to Admiral King, Walter Winchell, the powerful gossipmonger, dropped a little tidbit in his national column that inferred an ex-ambassador's son was the "romantic target of a suspected Nazi spy, and Pa no like."

Hoover, Admiral King and the ambassador immediately began damage control. The next day, on January 13, 1942, Jay received orders that he was being transferred to the Sixth Naval District, Charleston, South Carolina. More than a decade later, Jay described the event. "They shagged my ass down to South Carolina because I was going around with a Scandinavian blonde, and they thought she was a spy!"

Inga took the train to Charleston to visit Jay for the weekend of January 24. She checked into the Fort Sumter Hotel (1 King Street) under the name of Barbara White. Neither she nor Jay was seen on the streets for the rest of the weekend. She returned to Charleston the weekend of February 9, again registered as Barbara White. FBI agents followed the couple leaving their room for meals and they followed them to Sunday Mass. While they were out for a meal Saturday morning, agents planted listening devices in room 132 at the Fort Sumter Hotel and reported that "Jay and Mrs. Fejos engaged in sexual intercourse on a number of occasions." They also reported on a conversation about marriage.

Jay hated Charleston. His job was even more boring than the one in Washington, but at least D.C. had ample diversions. For Jay, Charleston was only a provincial backwater. In a letter, he complained about the city.

> Have I discussed Southerners with you? It's not so much that they say "hear" after every God damned remark — "now come and see us, hear?" — but it is the abots and oots — and all the rest of the shit that convinces me we should have let their bootucks go [at the time of the Civil War].

Meanwhile, back in Washington, Inga was bombarding Jay with letters and phone calls. She became aware of the FBI surveillance through Nils Blok, her former lover who worked for the Danish consulate. She resumed her affair with Blok, and he proposed marriage to Inga. She told him she must think over his offer.

During a phone call she informed Jay of the FBI surveillance of her. When she returned to Charleston on February 21, they tried to avoid the FBI by registering at two hotels, the Fort Sumter and the Francis Marion (387 King Street). Their room at the Francis Marion was planted with listening devices while they breakfasted downstairs on Saturday morning. The FBI transcript reported a serious discussion about marriage. Inga informed Jay that she had investigated the possibility of annulments (she would need two) as the only thing standing between them and a Catholic marriage.

On February 27 Jay had a long telephone conversation with his father, the ambassador, who told him of Mr. Blok and his marriage proposal to Inga. The next day Jay formally broke off the relationship with Inga.

In April 1943 Jay arrived on Guadalcanal, and on April 23, he took command of Patrol Boat 109. In November 1946, Jay was elected to the House of Representatives. In 1952, he was elected to the U.S. Senate and on January 20, 1961, Jay was inaugurated thirty-fifth president of the United States—John Fitzgerald Kennedy.

SINCLAIR GAS AND WHORE

Once there was a full-service gas station at the southwestern corner of Meeting and Market Streets. It was affiliated with the Sinclair Oil Company, the one with the dinosaur as a mascot. It was a generic looking gas station: gas pumps in the front, two service bays at one end of the building and a small convenience store/cashier area. For those who don't remember full-service gas stations, they operated like this: a car pulls up to the pump and the service attendant runs out to pump the gas, check the oil, air pressure and clean the windshield while the customer sits in the car. All for nineteen cents a gallon!

However, this was a FULL service gas station. Many of the customers (usually dressed in a naval or Air Force uniform) arrived without a car. They would purchase an overpriced bottle of Coke (about twenty dollars) and walk into the "service" area. There was always a big Cadillac in one of the service bays, parked over one of the lifts. The customer would carry the Coke into the "service" bay and climb into the back seat of the Caddy, where he would be joined by one of the female "service" attendants. Another attendant would lift the Caddy in the air.

Ten minutes later, the lift would be lowered and the man would exit the backseat and be on his merry way.

Later, when the city became serious about cleaning up the Market Street area, most of the clubs and bordellos were closed, and the "service" station went out of business. The building became the dispatch office for a cab company, but the side business remained. A streetwalking prostitute would pick up a customer and call a cab. The cab would pick up the couple and drive to the dispatch office. The driver parked in the service area, cranked the lift and took a ten-minute coffee break in the office, and then the driver would lower the cab and hit the streets, drop off the couple in the backseat and collect his fare.

J. Francis Brenner worked for the city at the time. According to his memoir *The Charleston Gospel*, he and the mayor once stood on the steps of Market Hall and watched the two hydraulic lifts "constantly in motion like a well coordinated seesaw, up and down."

The mayor shook his head at the ingenuity of it, and then ordered the activity stopped.

CHAPTER FIVE

THE QUEEN OF ANSONBOROUGH

Charleston is a city with Gothic tales, and what they don't know, they make up.

Dawn Langley Hall

harleston is not the center of the universe, but it should be. That is the persistent perception of many locals. It has been described as America's most aristocratic city and it may well be, since aristocracy in Charleston has as much to do with heritage, family and tradition as money. But money *never* hurts. In Charleston, money is the great equalizer. A family with the right name and heritage but no fortune will be welcomed as part of the fraternity, but not as quickly as a family with *no* heritage and *tons* of money.

Charleston has always worshiped its heritage and during the 1960s, the city was proud that it was completely out of step with the times. Most people had yet to install air conditioning, in a city where today living without air conditioning is unfathomable. It is a city where it is still possible to see A/C units sticking out the windows of $5 million mansions with tin roofs. America was going through a massive social and political upheaval with sexual and racial boundaries being destroyed on a daily basis, illustrated to the mass public on the nightly news. But Charleston was the proverbial ostrich with its regal head stuck in the sand.

In September 1962, a young English writer named Gordon Hall arrived in Charleston by chauffeured limousine. Gordon was accompanied by his parrot Marilyn and his two pedigreed Chihuahuas,

Nellie and Annabel-Eliza. Although Charleston was not known for its cold temperatures, Gordon had taken no chances and brought with him an electrically heated kennel for the dogs.

Gordon moved to arts-oriented Charleston with money to burn and a plan to take the city by storm. He had written several books, including biographies of Princess Margaret, Jacqueline Kennedy and a critically acclaimed volume on Mary Todd Lincoln. Gordon soon became part of the social elite in Charleston, throwing lavish parties and attending most of the exclusive social occasions in the city. He claimed friendship with Hollywood legends Bette Davis, Helen Hayes, Joan Crawford, writer Pearl S. Buck and boxer Sugar Ray Robinson. His godmother was famed British actress Dame Margaret Rutherford, who lavished motherly affection on him.

Many of the white Charleston elite accepted Gordon into their society due to his good manners, English pedigree and money. However, in the life story of Gordon Hall nothing is as it seems.

GORDON HALL

In one of his memoirs (yes, he wrote more than one), Gordon claimed he was born on October 16, 1937, (although the gravestone says 1922) in Heathfield, England. Gordon was the illegitimate child of fifteen-year-old Margie Hall Ticehurst and nineteen-year-old Jack Copper, who had accomplished the notorious feat of having three women pregnant at the same time. Gordon claimed in one of his autobiographies that his mother was so shunned by her family that she "locked herself in a darkened room for most of the nine months. One close and sadistic relative saw fit to kick her in the stomach."

Gordon's father, Jack, was the chauffeur of noted English poetess Vita Sackville-West who lived at Sissinghurst Castle, and his mother worked as a maid on the estate. From his earliest years, Gordon knew he was different. He was weak and had no interest in boyish pursuits. "I hated sport," he recalled, "and I remember always having to miss gym; I couldn't do the exercises." Whenever he was asked "Why don't you like girls?" Gordon would answer that he was too busy with his writing. Gordon's refuge from the world was writing. His first poem was published at age four and by age nine Gordon had a regular column in the Sussex *Express*.

Vita Sackville-West grew up in the largest house in England, Knole House, with 356 rooms and 52 staircases. In 1913, Vita married a young diplomat, Harold Nicolson, moved into Sissinghurst and the two began an unusual marriage. After giving birth to two children, Vita had several affairs with women, and Harold carried on with several men. The young Gordon was exposed to this wealthy, arts-oriented, sexually open, eccentric household off-and-on during his childhood. By the mid-1920s Vita had met the love of her life, the famous writer Virginia Woolf. Vita and Woolf personally encouraged Gordon, the son of their maid, to continue his writing.

One of Virginia Woolf's most famous books was *Orlando*. The story follows the three hundred-year life of a young man who romances his way through the sixteenth, seventeenth and eighteenth centuries until finally during the1800s he suddenly changes into a beautiful woman and continues to have romances (this time with men), and eventually gives birth. The young Gordon Hall was mesmerized by the book, and also by Woolf and Vita and their wealthy, unconventional lifestyle.

At age sixteen Gordon decided to leave England. He took a job for a year as a teacher on an Ojibwa Indian reservation in Ontario. He also got a job as the obituary writer for the Winnipeg *Free Press*. In 1955, he moved to the United States and worked as society editor for the Nevada, Missouri, *Daily Mail*. "They played it up that I was the first male society editor in the state of Missouri," he remembered. One year later Gordon was living in New York City where his modern morality play, *Saraband for a Saint*, received congratulations from actresses Joan Crawford and Helen Hayes and prompted an invitation from the archbishop of Canterbury.

While in Greenwich Village, Gordon stumbled into an art gallery where Isabel Whitney, a distant cousin, was having a show. Gordon and Isabel chatted and soon the sixty-year-old artist was so charmed by the young frail Englishman that she invited him to her house for tea. "Visiting Isabel's home was like entering some Tiffany cathedral," Gordon later wrote. Within a few weeks Gordon moved into the forty-room Whitney mansion at 12 West Tenth Street, taking over most of the top floor.

Isabel Whitney was a descendent of Eli Whitney, inventor of the cotton gin, and her father had been one of the founders of the Paterson Silk Industry in New Jersey. She also claimed kinship with William Penn and Gertrude Vanderbilt Whitney, one of the founders of the New York Museum of Modern Art. One of Isabel's childhood playmates had been the young Franklin D. Roosevelt. Through Isabel's patronage, Gordon was introduced to the elite of New York society, including English actress Dame Margaret Rutherford, who had recently won an Oscar as best supporting actress for the film *The V.I.P.s*. Like Isabel, Rutherford and her husband, Stringer Davis, were childless, and soon Gordon was calling them Mother Rutherford and Father Stringer. It was from the encouragement of these women that Gordon wrote his humorous memoir about his days on the Ojibwa reservation, *Me Papoose Sitter*. The book sold well and was optioned for the Broadway stage. Gordon soon became quite a personality in New York art and social circles.

One night Gordon and Isabel returned home from the opera to find a man crouched beneath their sidewalk stoop, drunk and freezing to death. They took him inside, warmed him, fed him, cleaned him and put him to bed. The next morning they discovered he was an Italian named Joseph Scaltro. To repay their kindness Joseph insisted on cooking their lunch. It turned out he was a good cook and Isabel invited him to move in. Soon, Joseph was sharing the top floor with Gordon and the two men became lovers. However, at some point, Joseph began to remove things out of Isabel's house and sell them to antique dealers. Gordon called Joseph a "charming scamp." It was not to be the last time Gordon was taken in by a charming scamp.

In 1959, Isabel was diagnosed with leukemia and for the next three years her condition worsened. Finally, in 1961, Gordon went looking for a house in the South with the intention of moving Isabel to the warmer climate to enjoy her final days. Gordon purchased a dilapidated mansion at 56 Society Street in Charleston. Two weeks later, on February 2, 1962, Isabel Whitney died in her bed in New York. When her will was read, Gordon inherited the New York mansion on West Tenth Street, art, jewelry, furniture and stock in Edison, General Electric, Standard Oil and Sears. All told it was more than $2 million. "I was surprised to have been left so much," he commented.

Gordon took the money, moved to Charleston by chauffeured limousine and restored the Society Street house in Ansonborough. He filled it with Chippendale furniture from the Whitney House. Other pieces included mirrors once owned by George Washington and bed steps belonging to Robert E. Lee. It was quite a coup for the bastard son of a fifteen-year-old English maid and a nineteen-year-old wayward chauffeur. Gordon was prepared to take Charleston society by storm.

"QUEENSBOROUGH"

Today Ansonborough is one of the city's most prestigious communities; however, when Gordon moved in, it had endured almost a century of decay. From its antebellum heyday, Ansonborough had taken a steady downward spiral so that by the 1960s, many of its mansions had been converted into tenements, flophouses and shabby apartments. There were small corner groceries and tobacco shops. The neighborhood was a mixture of blacks, blue-collar whites and a significant population of gay Charleston men: florists, hair stylists, decorators and restaurateurs.

One of Gordon's neighbors, Billy Camden, lived in Ansonborough in the 1960s. Camden was the owner of the gay bar Camden's Tavern. He claims that

> The gay couples really restored Ansonborough. I was on the Board of Directors for the Ansonborough Historic Foundation—it was made of 80 percent gay men! There was a gay couple or person in almost every home. They should have called it "Queensborough" instead.

During the antebellum days, Charleston's gay aristocracy lived within the social customs of the time. Gay sons were expected to move from the city so exposure of their sex habits would not embarrass their family. If they remained in Charleston, they must be completely discreet. During the 1960s most of the discreet men lived in Ansonborough. Even though the sexual revolution was in full flower throughout America, Charleston was a very repressed sexual society. It was a curious fact that many gay Charleston men were married with children. Gordon explained the custom this way: "So many of the men in Charleston, especially the married men, walk two roads. They marry a rich society matron that might not be good looking, and try to find somebody on the side." Well before the Clinton administration instituted the policy, Charleston society had a "don't ask-don't tell" rule of sexual behavior. If it could be ignored, most people didn't care.

Another of Gordon's "Queensborough" neighbors, Nicky, described 1960s gay life in Charleston.

> We lived as "out" as possible for that time period. We were socially active—visiting other gay couples for dinner, going to one of the

town's bars. We were also active in the larger Charleston community. Now, did other people know we were "gay"? Sure. Did we ever declare ourselves gay? No.

Ansonborough's reputation didn't rest only on the presence of a large gay population. There also were several houses of prostitution in the neighborhood. The first night in his new home Gordon was awakened at midnight by a group of drunken sailors. Seeing the lights from the chandeliers in the front room, the sailors had mistaken the newly restored home for a just-opened bordello.

Five doors to the west of Gordon's 56 Society Street address was the infamous Homo Hilton, home to drag queens, street people, drug dealers and sex hustlers of all types. Less than a block away was the Coffee Cup (presently Jestine's Kitchen at the corner of Meeting and Wentworth Streets), a twenty-four hour lunch counter where most customers showed up after 3:00 a.m. It was the favorite place for breakfast for the denizens of the Homo Hilton, their last stop before dawn.

Other social clubs included the Ratskellars on Court House Square. The Anchor was a mixed bar (gay and straight). The 49 Club was gay up front, mixed in the back, and gambling on the second floor. For the single gay man (not in a committed relationship) there was always ample opportunity to pick up men, particularly navy and Air Force men. The Battery and the Meeting Street bus stop, across the street from Citadel Square Baptist Church, were popular places to pick up cruising men.

Within a month Gordon had settled in his home and claimed that

The invitations from would-be matchmakers kept pouring in... leading hostesses gave suppers that I really dreaded. Always some poor husbandless girl was purposely placed beside me at the table. When I showed no particular interest in the feminine sex, there were those who decided that I must be homosexual.

He followed the custom of rich whites by hiring a black cook and butler. He also continued to write. He produced a biography of Princess Margaret, which was followed by *Golden Boats from Burma*, a book written about a relative of Isabel (Ann Judson), supposedly the first American woman to visit Burma. Next, Gordon wrote *Vinne Ream: The Story of the Girl Who Sculptured Lincoln*, a juvenile biography about the sculptor who created the statue of Lincoln that stands in the U.S. Capitol rotunda. This was followed by a book about Jackie Kennedy and *Mr. Jefferson's Ladies*, a portrait of the wife and daughters of Thomas Jefferson. Gordon later wrote *Lady Bird and Her Daughters*. All of Gordon's books were inspirational stories about women and self-discovery.

Billy Camden described his impressions of Gordon:

> *When he first came, everyone accepted him. He was small-framed, very effeminate guy with a thick English accent. At the beginning, the people connected with historic Ansonborough included him. But as soon as it got out what was going on—with all the blacks he entertained—that was the end of it! He would always be with a group of black, screaming queens. Charleston people would have nothing to do with him. He was an insult to the gay community; we were never friends.*

Nicky, another Ansonborough man, claimed that Gordon "patrolled Meeting Street at night. He loved black men almost as much as he liked old ladies with money." According to John Zeigler, longtime owner of the Book Basement in Charleston, Gordon would pick up "anybody who would have anal sex on him. He found men walking the streets, a lot of them on Meeting Street, in the area in front of Citadel Square Baptist Church. That was the cruising zone."

Julian Hayes claimed to have a one-night stand with Gordon in 1963. They met in the bathroom of the local Greyhound bus station. Hayes followed Gordon home, less than three blocks from the bus station, to Society Street. When Hayes was asked about Gordon's penis he commented, "I was very much impressed. You see, he was built much bigger than the average man. He had a penis that was enviable."

JOHN–PAUL SIMMONS

According to one account, Gordon met John-Paul Simmons in the late spring of 1967. John-Paul had a date with one of Gordon's young female black cooks. John-Paul arrived late, and the cook had already left. Gordon answered the door instead. "He was a little smiling man," Gordon wrote. "He never once asked for the cook." John-Paul returned the next day with an armful of flowers, and the secret affair began.

Secret because this was Charleston: the capital of slavery, the city that organized the Confederate States of America, the city that fired the first shot of the War Between the States; because in Charleston of 1967, blacks and whites did not engage in romantic sexual affairs, particularly a homosexual affair.

For several months the two carried on their furtive courtship. John-Paul was poor, black, brutish and uneducated. Joe Trott described John-Paul as not having "enough intelligence to get out of a shower of horse manure." On the other side, Gordon was rich, white, cultured and elite. He was frail, with fine features, gentle and quiet. An odder couple could hardly be found.

On December 11, 1967, Gordon Hall arrived at Johns Hopkins in Baltimore. During the five days he spent at the Gender Identity Clinic he met with seven doctors. By the end of the week Gordon was placed on estrogen tablets and told to dress as a woman immediately in preparation for sexual reassignment surgery. He returned to Charleston and while in the house he began to dress the part of a woman. He also underwent electrolysis to eliminate body hair.

Gordon began to tell everyone that he was really a woman, had always been a woman. He claimed that as a result of the kick in the belly his mother had endured during pregnancy he was born with a swollen clitoris that was misdiagnosed at birth as a penis by a poorly trained midwife. For years he had lived with the physical agony of cramps and blocked menstruation and that one morning his housekeeper arrived for work only to discover him lying in a pool of blood. He claimed he was rushed to the hospital and while the doctor was flushing out the blood he commented, "I can't understand why this is not fresh blood." Gordon claimed it was old menstrual blood that had been blocked for years.

Gordon's first public appearance as a woman was sitting in a car at a drive-in restaurant. Next, he went shopping at the Piggly Wiggly on Broad Street. Soon, he was making daily trips around the city in dresses and heels. However, there was a legal issue to deal with. Charleston had a city ordinance that prohibited one gender as going out in public dressed as the other. Gordon was afraid there would be an incident and he would be arrested. He hired a lawyer to alert the authorities that he was going though the process of having sex change surgery so he would not be arrested.

John-Paul began calling Gordon "Dawn"—to signal the dawn of their new life.

THE DAWN OF A NEW LIFE

On September 23, 1968, after successful surgery, Gordon woke from anesthesia in room B403 of Johns Hopkins Hospital as a woman: Dawn Pepita Langley Hall. Pepita was the nickname of Vita's grandmother, making the link between Vita, Virginia Woolf and Orlando public. The link between Gordon and Orlando was becoming more complete. Dawn said, "Gordon was no more as far as I was concerned. I destroyed every photograph, burnt all Gordon's clothes and had his name taken off my grandmother's gravestone."

Interviewed years later about the sex change surgery he performed on Gordon, Dr. Milton Edgerton commented about Gordon's clitoris and vagina claim. "We saw no evidence of that," Dr. Edgerton said. When asked if Gordon had a uterus and ovaries he said, "No, there was no suggestion of that."

Nevertheless, the transformation from Gordon to Dawn shocked genteel Charleston society. Biographer Jack Hitt remembered her as "small and thin, Dawn favored knee length skirts, a pillbox hat, and a Dippity-Do hairstyle—a dowdy doppelganger of Jackie Kennedy."

Dawn was welcomed back by many in Charleston society who tried to be sympathetic. After all, she still had a lot of money and good family background. There were persistent rumors of her affairs with several prominent Charleston men. The dinner invitations now included seating arrangements next to eligible bachelors.

But not everyone was so accommodating. Many who had welcomed Gordon into their homes now shunned Dawn when they passed her on the street or encountered her in the pews at St. Philip's church. Even so, the dissenters were in the minority...until Dawn and John-Paul announced their engagement.

At that time, the marriage of a black man and white woman was a crime in South Carolina. The state constitution prohibited the "marriage of a white person with a Negro or mulatto or a person who shall have one-eighth or more Negro blood." However, in 1967, the U.S. Supreme Court had ruled a similar Virginia law unconstitutional, so their marriage looked possible. Dawn hired a local African American attorney named Benard Fielding to help obtain the license. In the registry of Charleston County, license number 69-151 reads

THE QUEEN OF ANSONBOROUGH

HUSBAND:
Name: John-Paul Simmons
Sex: Male
Age: 21
Race: Negro

WIFE
Name: Dawn Pepita Langley Hall
Sex: Female
Age: 31
Race: White

Charleston's first interracial marriage of record was set for January 22, 1969.

First, however, three elderly Charleston society ladies came to Dawn's house. They brought an apple pie for Dawn and a watermelon for John-Paul. Why, they argued, couldn't she be like other proper white ladies who fell in love with their black butlers but properly married a white man? They told Dawn, "If, Miss Hall, you insist on going through with this disastrous union you will end up dead on a cooling couch."

When Dawn told John-Paul about the meeting, he asked, "Where's the watermelon?"

Jeremy Morrow, an Ansonborough resident, stated that "Back then, gay men did not *date* blacks, and we certainly didn't 'marry' them. Sex between black and white was *always* behind closed doors."

Another Charleston woman traveled all the way to England to beg Mother Rutherford to stop the marriage. True to form as a proper English lady, Mother Rutherford invited the Charleston woman to tea, but refused to intercede in Dawn's marriage. Word leaked out to the British press and on the following Sunday the London *News of the World* ran a headline that stated: "ROYAL BIOGRAPHER TO MARRY HER BUTLER."

Princess Margaret asked Mother Rutherford if it was true. "What would it matter, if he were a good butler?" Mother replied. She was later asked by *Time* magazine if she approved of the impending nuptials of her adopted daughter (son?). Mother replied, "Oh, I don't mind Dawn marrying a black man but I do wish she wasn't marrying a Baptist." She also told Dawn that "A man worth lying down with is worth standing up with."

MARRIAGE

On January 23, 1969 the *New York Times* wrote:

> *British-born Dawn Pepita Langley Hall, who was writer Gordon Langley Hall before a sex change, was married tonight to John-Paul Simmons, her Negro steward. The bride, an adopted daughter of Dame Margaret Rutherford, the actress, has given her age as 31. The groom is 22.*

In the Charleston *News and Courier*, the marriage was written up on the obituary page. John-Paul was hanged in effigy and several of their dogs were poisoned. Dawn (and Gordon) had always attended St. Philip's Episcopal Church in Charleston, the oldest Anglican congregation in America south of Virginia, established in 1680. A bomb threat to the church convinced Dawn to hold the ceremony in her home on Society Street.

On the day of the ceremony, the local radio stations alerted listeners that Charleston's wedding of the year (or *any* year) was to take place. Liz Smith, gossip columnist for the *Daily News*, called to find out if Dawn was going to be wearing the pearls that Mother Rutherford had given her. Joan Crawford sent a bouquet of yellow rosebuds and commented, "The heart knows why." Helen Hayes wrote Dawn a letter of encouragement. "There is no racial or religious prejudice among people of the theatre." Mother Rutherford insisted, "No wedding march for you. I want 'The Battle Hymn of the Republic.'" The "Battle Hymn" was a Civil War anthem for Union troops, sung as they marched through the defeated South. Dawn chose the song purposely to show contempt for the Charleston white elite that had abandoned her.

A crowd gathered on Society Street. Curious onlookers mixed on the street with dozens of reporters, everybody shouting, jeering and cheering. There was a heavy police presence, alert for any violence. Dawn recalled that "the street was packed, their bodies rippling like waves." According to Joe Trott, the florist for the wedding, "People were hanging out the windows…cameras were rolling. The police department was there, the fire department. I was so scared I would get shot. I was trying to get on a solid wall in case anybody was a sniper from one of the rooms across the street."

For the ceremony, Dawn wore a floor-length dress with appliquéd lace flowers. Two five-year old boys carried her ten-foot train. The dogs wore corsages. After the minister pronounced them "husband and wife," the couple kissed for thirty-seven seconds. Then they stepped onto their piazza to wave to the cheering (and jeering) crowd.

Jet magazine ran a feature about Dawn and her African American husband. *Newsweek* ran a page-long story about the "anguished transsexual" and her "Negro garage mechanic."

Two weeks later, a second, far grander wedding was held in Hastings, England, arranged by Mother Rutherford, who insisted that her daughter be properly married in a church. Mother had been outraged that Dawn was not given permission for a church marriage in Charleston. "There is more than one way to skin a cat," she stated, and called the archbishop of Canterbury. The ceremony was held at gothic stone St. Clements Church in Hastings and was hosted by Mother Rutherford. There were so many photographers that they filled the choir loft. Following the ceremony, Dawn and John-Paul attended a tea at the home of the archbishop of Canterbury. The British tabloid *The People* ran a month-long serial about Dawn's life. The story began with this spectacular claim:

> *A remarkable FACT had now been established. At The People's instigation Mrs. Simmons was examined by one of Britain's most eminent gynecologists at his Harley Street surgery. He stated: "Mrs. Dawn Simmons was probably wrongly sexed at birth. She has the genital organs of a woman capable of normal sexual intercourse, and she is capable of having a baby." On the evidence of the report it is not impossible that she could become pregnant.*

The newspaper withheld the name of the "eminent gynecologist."

When the couple returned from London, a crate of wedding gifts had been delivered to their front yard. During the night the crate was ransacked and all the wedding gifts were destroyed. The next morning the local police chief arrived to personally ticket them for "littering and having debris blocking the sidewalk."

The harassment continued. John-Paul was shot at three times on the street. Dawn was run down on Anson Street by an unknown driver, injuring her shoulder. The telephone rang incessantly with crank calls and death threats. Several callers delighted in telling Dawn they had seen John-Paul "consorting with other women," which was true, since he did have several other girlfriends. Dawn's Doberman pinscher, Charley, was poisoned and the basset hound, Samantha, was killed by a hit-and-run driver.

Dawn had spent an incredible amount of money in a twelve-month period: two weddings, a trip to Europe and the Ford Thunderbird she had purchased as John-Paul's wedding gift. When he totaled that car, she bought him a second, and a year later, she purchased a *third* Thunderbird. Dawn refurbished her mother-in-law's house. John-Paul also told Dawn he had decided he wanted to fish for a living, so she bought him a twenty-seven foot trawler, which was used for parties. The boat ended up abandoned in the marsh along the Cooper River.

Dawn then began to tell everyone that she and John-Paul were hoping to have a baby.

Terry Fox, a former neighbor, remembers:

> *I came to Charleston in the late 1960s and moved to number 52 Society Street...two doors down from Dawn. I was twenty-three and comparatively naive. At the time, part of me thought of Dawn as being a worldly, sophisticated person, who wouldn't have anything to do with me. And then there was the freak-show part of her...But she was always very gracious and friendly.*
>
> *After one year of marriage, Dawn to decided to give herself a first anniversary party. I walked in...and nobody was in sight. The place was stenchful, and overrun with dogs. Suddenly, Dawn descended the staircase, dressed in a full length, form-fitting red brocade dress, with long sleeves and wearing some kind of tiara.*

According to Fox, the dining room was set up with beautiful silver pieces, tarnished, and the table was laden with lunchmeat in plastic wrappers from Piggly Wiggly: Oscar Meyer bologna, Kraft American cheese slices and pickle loaf salami. Less than a dozen people attended, including several of Dawn's gay friends and John-Paul's mother.

In the meantime, John-Paul was continually unfaithful and fathered an illegitimate son. He was diagnosed with chronic schizophrenia, which often caused delusions and hallucinations. John-Paul began hearing voices and having conversations with a three-eyed woman from Mars he called "Big Girl." Like other sufferers John-Paul began to experience thought interruptions such as laughing at a sad moment or becoming completely disoriented to his surroundings.

Dawn's extravagant life proved too much for Charleston's closeted gay community. Her interracial marriage also sparked racism in the black community. As Jack Hitt wrote, "Typically when one crosses forbidden lines: interracial marriage, announcing one is gay, taking a lover from another religion or class, or even changing one's sex at least there is a community on the other side waiting for you. But Dawn charged across so many borders at once that she slipped into a country where she was the only inhabitant."

There was more trouble. In April 1971, the bank foreclosed on 56 Society Street. Dawn claimed that due to a mail strike in England she was not receiving her royalty checks. A friend, Richia Atkinson Barloga, who lived south of Broad Street, offered to pay the mortgage in full, but according to Dawn, Richia disappeared, literally. Richia later claimed to have been drugged by a man and taken to a local motel. She resurfaced ten days later after the Society Street house had been sold at auction. Dawn and John-Paul moved into a rented house at 15 Thomas Street, a far cry from their upscale Ansonborough address. Dawn carried her precious antiques and artwork into a house with twenty-seven broken windows. Many in Charleston were smug in their assessment, a satisfying "I told you so!" in their minds, if not on their lips.

Then Dawn made an amazing announcement. She claimed she was pregnant with John-Paul's baby.

WHERE'D THAT BABY COME FROM?

For several months during the spring and summer of 1971, Dawn walked the streets of Charleston wearing maternity clothes. Terry Fox, neighbor and guest at the first anniversary party, recalled seeing Dawn walking the streets in maternity clothes and flat shoes. But others didn't believe it. Some claimed she had a big belly beneath her dress one day and a flat stomach the next. Someone claimed to see a military surplus blanket stuffed beneath Dawn's dress. "She became something of a laughingstock," Fox recalled.

Anna Montgomery worked at a baby store on King Street and waited on Dawn. Anna claimed in the *Charleston Chronicle* that when Dawn walked into the store to make a purchase, the women laughed. She looked like a pregnant woman, Anna said, but "he forgot to tie down the strings of a pillowcase stuffed with cotton."

Dawn called those comments "wicked." "I did use cotton wool pads," she claimed, "but because of the burning in the breasts."

She tried to interest newspaper and magazine editors in her pregnancy story, but no one cared. She was no longer an exotic story; more often she inspired pity. She was convinced that white Charleston wanted to kill her unborn half-black child. She claimed there were numerous threats against her, so she decided to move seven hundred miles north to Philadelphia to give birth at the University of Pennsylvania hospital—or maybe to better hide whatever deception she was trying to pull. John-Paul remained in Charleston, in the housing project home of his girlfriend and mother of his son.

According to a birth certificate on file at the Department of Health Vital Statistics in the commonwealth of Pennsylvania, on October 17, 1971, Natasha Marginell Manugault Paul Simmons was born. Dawn herself gets the birth date of her "daughter" wrong in her last autobiography, citing it was October 15. The first time John-Paul saw Natasha he commented, "Whoever saw a blue-eyed nigger?"

After her return to Charleston, Dawn pushed Natasha up and down the streets in an old-fashioned British baby carrier just like the one the Queen had for Prince Charles. She kept the birth certificate handy to flash at all doubters. Many were not convinced, particularly men like Julian Hayes, who had once described Gordon's penis as "enviable." Even John-Paul wasn't impressed. He knew *exactly* where Natasha came from: one of his girlfriends.

"I'd been going with her for eight months—constantly had sex, sex, sex, all the time with this girl," he said. "She was about twenty-three. She got pregnant." John-Paul claimed that the girl's daddy knew Dawn wanted a baby, and the daddy didn't want his daughter to have an illegitimate daughter with a black man. When the girl went into labor, the girl checked into Roper Hospital as "Mrs. Simmons" at Dawn's direction. Dawn gave the daddy one thousand dollars for the baby. Dawn flew to Philadelphia with the South Carolina birth certificate listing "Mrs. John-Paul Simmons" as mother of the child. Dawn showed up at the Pennsylvania vital statistics office with the infant in her arms and paperwork in her hand bearing her name.

Dawn's announcement of the birth of her daughter became the fodder for TV comedians Dan Rowan and Dick Martin, hosts of the wildly popular *Rowan & Martin's Laugh-In*, a show with more than forty million viewers. The opening monologue contained the following exchange:

THE QUEEN OF ANSONBOROUGH

Dan Rowan: *News flash: Charleston, South Carolina. Noted transsexual Dawn Simmons has just given birth to a daughter.*
Dick Martin: *We can only hope she grows up to be half the man her mother was.*

Dawn moved to upstate New York and rented a run-down, ten-room mansion in the Catskills. The *New York Times* published a story under the headline "TRANSSEXUAL STARTING NEW LIFE IN CATSKILLS." Less than year later, however, the *Times* filed a follow-up story that read

> *Today, the house is an empty wreck. The owner has sued for $800 in rent. As of last week, the Simones [sic] were on welfare, living in a local hotel. Cash from the book that Mrs. Simmons was reported to be writing did not materialize. With no money for fuel, the family moved out "in the dead of winter"…and the pipes froze and burst, flooding the premises.*

Dawn's writing career had been reduced to writing for *The National Enquirer*. John-Paul was in and out of mental health facilities, popping in and out of her life. "I would never desert him," Dawn said. "I always see that he has clothes, pocket money and everything he needs."

In 1995, Dawn published her third memoir, *Dawn: A Charleston Legend*. Her first two, *Man Into Woman* and *All For Love*, had been published more than twenty years before. For several years she had been living in North Charleston in a federally subsidized housing project. She was also the devoted grandmother of Natasha's three children. She published a novel, *She-Crab Soup*, which managed to sell seventeen copies in its first year of publication.

Dawn Pepita Langley Hall Simmons, the former Gordon Hall, died quietly on September 18, 2000, of effects from Parkinson's disease. The funeral took place at the chapel of the J. Henry Stuhr Funeral Home. Natasha placed a misleading announcement in the newspaper so that the funeral would not become a media circus. Her body was cremated and divided into three equal parts: one-third to a friend in New Hampshire, a third to England and the rest to Natasha. It was the end of a real-life Orlando as Dawn passed from a country in which she was the only citizen to the more populous world of the dead.

TRANSCRIPTION OF THE CHARLESTON BLUE BOOK

Cover
The Blue Book
Exposition Number
Charleston, S.C.
1902 /Price 25 Cents

Inside Cover
MISS ELSIE CAMERON
No. 11 Beresford Street
First-class in every particular

Page 1
MISS MATTIE SHERMAN
No. 46 Mazyck Street
The following young ladies solicit your acquaintance:
Miss Vina DeVon
Miss Fannie Harris
Miss Stella Lewis
Miss Leona Harris
Miss Marie Hollander
Miss Lillie Carson

Page 2

Here's to the grape and here's to the wine
Here's to you girls, if you'll be mine

I'll be faithful if you'll be true
And I'll never leave my happy home for you
❀ ❀ ❀ ❀ ❀

There was but one girl in all this world of ours
When Eve ate the apple in the garden of the flowers
Eve was clothed in fig leaves, Adam none at all
But he knew he would see the picture when the leaves began to fall

Page 3
MISS IRENE WARNER
Nos. 3 and 5 Clifford Street
Has associated herself with the following bright and entertaining ladies:
Miss Gladys Greye
Miss Ethel McDonald
Miss Bertha Lippencott

Page 4

The boy stood on the burning deck,
With his back against the mast
"I will not stir one step," he said
"'Till Oscar Wilde has passed."
❀ ❀ ❀ ❀ ❀

Here's to you as good as you are;
Here's to me as bad as I am;
But as good as you are, and as bad as I am
I am as good as you are as bad as I am.
❀ ❀ ❀ ❀ ❀

Into this world we come naked and bare
We go through it with trouble and care
We die, we go—we know not where
But if we're thoroughbreds here,
We'll be thoroughbreds there.

Page 5
No. 49 Mazyck Street
MISS BELLE PERCIVAL
Will be pleased to make your acquaintance
And introduce for your amusement:
Miss Blanche Clark

Miss Marie Wallace
Miss Audrey Hasting

Page 6
It was a hot Sunday morning in July. Still a large congregation had assembled for divine worship. Due to the unusual heat the good minister decided not to preach a regular sermon, but to read the Ten Commandments and offer a few comments as he passed by.
When he reached the Seventh Commandment, "Thou Shalt Not Commit Adultery," one of the good old deacons struck the side of his pew with a loud thump. This particular act was noticed by the minister. Fearing that Brother Jones may require his assistance, the minister went over after the service and asked why he had struck the blow when that particular Commandment was read.
Deacon Jones replied, "Why, I suddenly remembered where I left my umbrella."

Page 7
MISS AGNES CAMPBELL
No. 9 Beresford Street
Respectfully invites you to call and be entertained by:
Miss Nettie Davis
Miss Ridia Brown
Miss Ruth Allen
Miss Willie Black
Miss Marie Nash
Miss Helen Crawford
Miss Mae Vernon
Miss Violet Hastings

Page 8
Wine, women and song
Make the world run long
The first to please, the second to tease
And the three to make a man go wrong

Page 9
Your visit to Charleston will not be complete unless you call at
No. 37 Archdale Street

Where MISS MARIE MANNING will see that you are properly entertained.
Among the young ladies are:
Miss Marie Taylor
Miss May Odell
Miss Beatrice Mentell
MISS IDA LAVELLE
Miss May Clark
Miss Lettie Pick

Pages 10 and 11
Index of Ladies
Allen, Miss Ruth, 9 Beresford Street
Black, Miss Willie, 9 Beresford Street
Brooks, Miss Sadie, 14 Coming Street
Brown, Miss Ridia, 9 Beresford Street
Campbell, Miss Agnes, 9 Beresford Street
Cameron, Miss Elsie, 11 Beresford Street
Carson, Miss Lillie, 46 Mazyck Street
Clark, Miss Blanche, 49 Mazyck Street
Clark, Miss Mae, 37 Archdale Street
Crawford, Miss Helen, 9 Beresford Street
Davis, Miss Nettie, 9 Beresford Street
De Von, Miss Vina, 46 Mazyck Street
Greye, Miss Gladys, 3 and 5 Clifford Street
Harris, Miss Fannie, 46 Mazyck Street
Harris, Miss Leona, 46 Mazyck Street
Hasting, Miss Audrey, 49 Mazyck Street
Hastings, Miss Violet, 9 Beresford Street
Hollander, Miss Marie, 46 Mazyck Street
Lavelle, Miss Ida, 37 Archdale Street
Lewis, Miss Stella, 46 Mazyck Street
Lippencott, Miss Bertha, 3 and 5 Clifford Street
Mallard, Miss Marion, 14 Coming Street
Manning, Miss Marie, 37 Archdale Street
McDonald, Miss Ethel, 3 and 5 Clifford Street
Mentell, Miss Beatrice, 37 Archdale Street
Nash, Miss Marie, 9 Beresford Street
Odell, Miss May, 37 Archdale Street

Percival, Miss Belle, 49 Mazyck Street
Pick, Miss Lettie, 37 Archdale Street
Sherman, Miss Mattie, 46 Mazyck Street
Randolph, Miss Edith, 14 Coming Street
Taylor, Miss Marie, 37 Archdale Street
Vernon, Miss Mae, 9 Beresford Street
Wallace, Miss Marie, 49 Mazyck Street
Warner, Miss Irene, 3 and 5 Clifford Street

Page 12 (inside back cover)
MISS EDITH RANDOLPH
Assisted by Miss Marion Mallard and Miss Sadie Brooks will try and make things pleasant for you if you call at No. 14 Coming Street

BIBLIOGRAPHY

A. MANUSCRIPTS

Charleston Directory 1866. Compiled by Burke and Roinset. New York: M.B. Brown and Company, 1866.

Chicora Foundation, "Charleston's Other Side." Vol. 8, No. 4, 1995.

Interview with Raven McDavid, AFS 14218:A3, Archive of Folk Culture, Library of Congress.

Michel, Dr. William Middleton. "Report of the Examination of the Body of Francis Warrington Dawson." Charleston: South Carolina Historical Society.

Preservation Progress, Preservation Society of Charleston. "Early Taverns In Charleston." May 1971.

B. NEWSPAPERS AND MAGAZINES

Abbeville Press
Atlantic Monthly
Charleston City Gazette
Charleston Courier
Charleston Evening Post

Charleston Magazine

Charleston Mercury

Charleston News and Courier

Charleston Post and Courier

Charleston Times

Chicago Tribune

"Dawn Langley Simmons, Flamboyant Writer, Dies at 77." *GAIN Digest*, September 24, 2000.

Grafton, Samuel. "The Loneliest Man In Town." *Collier's*, April 29, 1950.

Hitt, Jack. "The Legend of Dawn." *GQ*, October 1998, 268–278.

Lancaster (SC) *Ledger*

Leland, Jack. "History of the Unholy City," *Charleston Magazine*. May-June 1975.

Lowcountry News and Review

Newberry (SC) *Herald*

New York Times

Simmons, Dawn Langley. "Real Lives: The Woman Brought Up As A Man," *Marie Claire*, February 1996, 54, 56, 58.

Walsh, Walter Richard. "Edmund Egan: Charleston's Rebel Brewer." *South Carolina Historical Magazine*, October 1955.

C. OTHER SOURCES

Abbott, Geoffrey. *A Macabre Miscellany*. London: Virgin Books, 2004.

Ball, Edward. *Peninsula of Lies: The True Story of Mysterious Birth and Taboo Love*. New York: Simon & Schuster, 2004.

Bland, Sidney. *Preserving Charleston's Past, Shaping Its Future: The Life and Times of Susan Pringle Frost*. Westport, CT: Greenwood Press, 1994.

Breibart, Solomon. *Explorations of Charleston's Jewish History*. Charleston: The History Press, 2005.

Brenner, J. Francis. *The Charleston Gospel According To St. Michael, St. Philip and St. John*. Johns Island, SC: Old Codger's, 2001.

Chesnut, Mary Boykin. *A Diary From Dixie*. Gloucester, MA: Peter Smith, 1961.

Clark, E. Culpepper. *Francis Warrington Dawson and the Politics of Restoration: South Carolina, 1874–1889*. Tuscaloosa: University of Alabama Press, 1980.

BIBLIOGRAPHY

Davis, Kenneth C. *Don't Know Much About the Civil War*. New York: William Morrow and Company, 1996.

Donehue, J. Douglas. *Charleston on the Air*. Columbia: The R.L. Bryan Company, 2000.

Edgar, Walter. *South Carolina: A History*. Columbia: University of South Carolina Press, 1998.

Fraser, Walter J. *Charleston! Charleston! The History of a Southern City*. Columbia: University of South Carolina Press, 1989.

Hosmer, Charles B. Jr. *Preservation Comes of Age: From Williamsburg to the National Trust, 1926–1949*. 2 vols. Charlottesville: University Press of Virginia for the National Trust for Historic Preservation Press, 1981.

Huggins, Phillip K. *The South Carolina Dispensary*. Columbia: Sandlapper Press, 1971.

Jablonski, Edward, and Lawrence D. Stewart. *The Gershwin Years*. New York: Doubleday and Company, 1973.

Jacoby, Mary Moore, ed. *The Churches of Charleston and the Lowcountry*. Columbia: University of South Carolina Press, 1994.

Lander, Ernest Mcpherson. *A History of South Carolina, 1865–1960*. Columbia: University of South Carolina Press, 1970.

Leamer, Laurence. *The Kennedy Men, 1901–1963*. New York: Harper Collins, 2001.

Leiding, Harriette Kershaw. *Charleston: Historic and Romantic*. Philadelphia: J.B. Lippincott Company, 1931.

Leland, Jack. *62 Famous Dwelling Houses of Charleston, South Carolina*. Charleston: Post-Courier Booklet, 1970.

Longacre, Edward G. *Gentleman and Solder: The Extraordinary Life of General Wade Hampton*. Nashville: Rutledge Hill Press, 2003.

McDougal, Walter A. *Freedom Just Around The Corner: A New American History 1585–1828*. New York: Harper Collins, 2004.

Moore, Margaret H. *Complete Charleston: A Guide To The Architecture, History, and Gardens of Charleston and the Low Country*. Charleston: TM Photography, 2000.

Pease, Jane H., and William H. Pease. *Ladies, Women & Wenches*. Chapel Hill: University of North Carolina Press, 1990.

Perret, Geoffrey. *Jack: A Life Like No Other*. New York: Random House, 2001.

Phillips, Caryl. *The Atlantic Sound*. New York: Alfred A. Knopf, 2000.

Pike, James S. *The Prostrate State*. New York: Loring and Mussey, 1935.

Poston, Jonathon H. *The Buildings of Charleston: A Guide to the City's Architecture*. Columbia: University of South Carolina Press, 1997.

Ravenel, Beatrice St. J., ed. *Charleston Murders*. New York: Duell, Sloan & Pierce, 1947.

Renhehan, Edward J. Jr. *The Kennedys at War: 1937–1945*. New York: Random House, 2002.

Rhyne, Nancy. *Murder in the Carolinas*. Greensboro, NC: Avisson Press, 1998.

Rogers, George C. *Charleston in the Age of the Pinckneys*. Columbia: University of South Carolina Press, 1980. First published 1969 by University of Oklahoma Press.

Rosen, Robert. *A Short History of Charleston*. Columbia: University of South Carolina Press, 1992.

———. *Confederate Charleston*. Columbia: University of South Carolina Press, 1992.

Sears, James T. *Lonely Hunters: An Oral History of Lesbian and Gay Southern Life, 1948–1968*. Boulder, CO: Westview Press, 1997.

BIBLIOGRAPHY

Simmons, Dawn Langley. *All For Love.* Star Books, 1975.

———. *Dawn: A Charleston Legend.* Charleston: Wyrick & Company, 1995.

———. *Man Into Woman: A Transsexual Autobiography.* Icon Books, 1970.

Smith, Alice R. Huger, and D.E. Huger. *The Dwelling Houses of Charleston, South Carolina.* New York: Lippincott, 1917.

Thompson, Henry T. *Ousting the Carpetbagger From South Carolina.* Columbia: R.L. Bryan Company, 1927.

Thompson, Jack. *Charleston at War: The Photographic Record 1860–1865.* Gettysburg, PA: Thomas Publications, 2000.

Trinkley, Michael, and Debi Hacker. *The Other Side of Charleston: Archeological Survey of the Saks Fifth Avenue Location.* Charleston: Chicora Foundation, 1995.

Wallace, David Duncan. *South Carolina: A Short History, 1520–1948.* Columbia: University of South Carolina Press, 1951.

Waring, J. Waties. *The Remininisces of J. Waties Waring.* New York: Columbia University, 1956.

Williams, Alfred B. *Hampton and His Red Shirts: South Carolina's Deliverance in 1876.* Charleston: Walker, Evans & Cogswell Company, 1935.

Williams, Arthur V. Jr. *Tales of Charleston 1930s.* Charleston: College of Charleston Library in association with the Jewish Historical Society of South Carolina, 1999.

Williams, Jack Kenny. *Vogues in Villainy.* Columbia: University of South Carolina Press. 1959.

———. *Crime and Punishment in South Carolina, 1790–1860.* Ann Arbor: University of Michigan Dissertation Services, 1953.

Yarbarough, Tinsley. *A Passion for Justice: J.Waties Waring and Civil Rights.* London: Oxford University Press, 1987.

ABOUT THE AUTHOR

Mark R. Jones is a ninth-generation native of South Carolina. He is a licensed City of Charleston tour guide, conducting carriage tours for Palmetto Carriage and daytime history and nighttime ghost tours for Bulldog Walking Tours. Mark is also one of a select group of guides who conducts the Dark Side of Charleston Tour for Bulldog: the tour that inspired the writing of the *Wicked Charleston* books. The Dark Side is the only non-ghost nighttime tour in Charleston. On average, Mark conducts twenty tours a week, about one thousand per year.

He is the author of *Wicked Charleston: The Dark Side of the Holy City*, which covers the history of the founding of Charles Towne from a unique perspective: drinking, prostitution and murder. The Charleston *Post and Courier* called the book "a solid (if tipsy) foundation for the revelry to come." *Wicked Charleston, Volume 2* is the continuation of that revelry.

In his free time, Mark is always on the prowl for new salacious stories about Charleston. Information about Mark, his books, tours, personal blog and speaking engagements can be found at his web site: www.wickedcharleston.net.